WINE

William Sharp
is a free-lance writer
living in southern California

Joseph Martin
is a wine consultant for restaurants
and owner of a wine shop

WINE

How to Develop Your Taste & Get Your Money's Worth

WILLIAM J. SHARP
JOSEPH MARTIN

Illustrations by Charles C. Pitcher

A SPECTRUM BOOK

PRENTICE-HALL, INC., Englewood Cliffs, New Jersey

Library of Congress Cataloging in Publication Data

SHARP, WILLIAM J.
    Wine: How to develop your taste & get your money's worth.

    (A Spectrum Book)
    Includes index.
        1. Wine and wine making. 2. Wine tasting.
I. Martin, Joseph, (date)-   joint author.
II. Title.
TP548.S525   641.2'2   76-1866
ISBN O-13-957746-7
ISBN   O-13-957738-6 pbk.

A SPECTRUM BOOK

10   9   8   7   6   5   4   3   2   1

Printed in the United States of America

Prentice-Hall International, Inc., *London*
Prentice-Hall of Australia Pty., Limited, *Sydney*
Prentice-Hall of Canada, Ltd., *Toronto*
Prentice-Hall of India Private, Limited, *New Delhi*
Prentice-Hall of Japan, Inc., *Tokyo*
Prentice-Hall of South-East Asia Private, Limited, *Singapore*

Contents

Preface

Are you a bit insecure when it comes to buying a bottle of wine? Do you have the feeling that you don't know enough about it to make an intelligent selection? Are you confused about "good years" and "bad years," and wondering what makes the difference anyway? In short, are you *intimidated* by wine?

If the answer to any or all of these questions is "yes," then this book is for you.

Our experience tells us that many people in the United States *are* intimidated by wine—by the complexity of wine labels, by magazine articles and books that obscure the subject rather than make it clear, by the jargon used by the so-called wine experts, indeed, by the whole mystique that has developed around buying and drinking the "nectar of the gods."

Hardly a day goes by without someone asking us about vintage years, and secretly wondering in the meantime if it really matters at all. We hear frequent complaints about expensive bottles of wine tasting terrible, and our customers want to know why.

It is an absurd state of affairs—absurd because there is absolutely no reason why something as pleasant as drinking a glass of wine should have become so esoteric and complex. Yet very few people are secure in their knowledge about wine. Confusion reigns.

Take, for example, the daily situation in fine restaurants all across the country. Presented with a wine list, many people glance at it, shrug their shoulders, and order the house wine, simply because they are threatened by the unknown labels and the French and German words that confront them. Even worse, when a wine steward opens a bottle and pours a sip for you to taste, then peers down his nose at you while he waits for your nod of approval, it is only human to be intimidated and to accept the wine without question.

The general impression is that you have to be a wine expert to make sense of it all. But take it from us—you do not have to be an expert to sort it all out. All you need is some basic information and a willingness to taste various wines in order to determine which you like and which you do not.

That is what we are going to give you—basic information. We are going to tell you how to select wines, how to store them, how to blend them for your own special delight, and how to know what you are getting when you buy a bottle of wine. We are even going to tell you how to host your own wine-tasting party.

What we are *not* going to give you is a lot of extraneous information. We are not going to pad this book, as most wine authors do, by waxing eloquent over the beauty of a number of obscure wines. Nor will we burden you with a lot of pompous-sounding, and essentially meaningless, technical information. And we promise we will not send you off on a search for some mysterious wine whose name no one has ever heard of.

We are going to ask you to stop listening to the wine snobs, to put away the notion that inexpensive wine is undrinkable, and to start letting your own taste be the judge. Remember: we are not setting out to make you a wine expert; we just want you to be able to enjoy wine a whole lot more than you have in the past. So we wish you good reading . . . and good tasting!

We would like to acknowledge our debt to Batista Gininni, who initially interested us in wine many years ago. Thanks to our wives for their encouragement, to Brady McManus for his knowledgable explanations, and to the many friends whose interest we appreciate.

WINE

Making a Start

Let's say you are the typical American who enjoys a glass of wine. You have tasted some wines you liked and some you did not, but whether you have been drinking wine for six months or six years, you have always had the feeling that if you had been able to afford a "better" wine, you would have enjoyed it more.

You are also a bit confused by the information you have collected over the years from the so-called "wine experts"—confused to the degree that you no longer know what to believe. The feeling persists that there is some mystery involved in selecting a wine, and that if only you could collar one of those wine authorities for an evening, you could unravel the mystery.

In all probability, you are willing to admit to yourself, if not to your friends, that deep down inside your brain you really don't know much at all about wine.

Let's take a look at the way you buy wine. Your normal procedure has been to saunter into a store that sells wine, look around a bit, spot a label you have heard of (probably through advertising), and make a spur-of-the-moment decision to buy that kind. After all, you need some wine. Perhaps the boss is coming to your

1

house for dinner in about two hours. Or maybe you are all out of that cheap red table wine that *almost* went well with every meal. Or maybe you simply want to "mellow out" for the evening. Whatever the reason, you have to buy some wine.

That was the way you went about it in the past. Lately, however, you have decided to go at this whole thing in a more systematic way. You have heard all the rantings and ravings about "great" wines and you want to get in on the fun.

Your first step was to go out and buy a book in the hope that it would explain to you all the things you need to know in order to make an intelligent selection. Unfortunately, the book did not help. It seemed to be written in Martian, while all you studied in school was Sanskrit.

You tried another tactic. A woman with whom you work calls herself a wine connoisseur, and you went to her for advice, thinking she could give you some help. But wrong again. She gave you some advice, all right, but when you paid a visit to your local liquor and wine merchant, you discovered it would take two-thirds of your weekly grocery allowance just to buy two bottles of what she recommended.

Then, just at the moment you decided the whole thing was a farce, old lucky you spotted a store clerk waving a featherduster over some exotic-looking wine bottles. Figuring that because he works there he must know something, you sidled up to him and asked for some help. But when he pointed you in the direction of *his* favorite wine, a heavily advertised brand of apple wine, you knew you were on the wrong track again.

2   If all this sounds familiar to you, if it rings a

tiny bell inside your head, do not be discouraged.
You are not alone. People all over the United
States have been so intimidated by wine snobs
(who exist in countless numbers) that there are
millions of us in this same boat. Our native
intelligence tells us that something as simple as
buying and drinking a bottle of wine just cannot
be that complicated. But on the other hand,
there is that esoteric quality associated with
wine. The result is, we don't know which way to
turn.

To solve the problem, the very first thing
you have to do is forget most of what you have
read and heard about wine. Probably 95 percent
of it was wrong. What we ask you to do is open
your mind, forget about any principles you
think you know, forget that aura of mystery you
think surrounds wine. Simply make up your
mind to be open and flexible, and we will start
you on the road to a greater enjoyment of wine
than you ever thought possible.

But, prepare for some surprises. Are you
ready for the first step? Here it is: start your
wine education by buying the most inexpensive
wines first!

That's right, the least expensive. And when
we say *in*expensive, we really mean it. We mean
you should pick out some of the cheap brands
that sell for about three bucks a gallon jug and
try them. Then, and only then, should you work
your way into the more expensive wines. For a
beginner, this is the only way to go.

Does this sound crazy to you? Let us
illustrate what we are talking about. There is a
very fine French restaurant in our area—it is
small, but worthy of its good reputation. A
"house wine"—a wine you buy in a carafe

without a label—is served there which draws raves from both the gourmet critics and most of the patrons. And do you know what this wine is? It is a California wine that costs less than $2.50 a gallon. We know because we sell this restaurant its wine.

We do not point this out to belittle people's tastes, nor to play one-upmanship with the gourmet writers. We simply want to make the point that cheap wine can be good wine. You must admit that $2.50 per gallon is pretty cheap, and we think you have to agree that if a wine is good enough for the newspaper restaurant critics to rave about, it must have something going for it.

The wine industry generally supports the notion that cheap wine cannot be any good. We ask you not to believe it. The wine industry does not even want the word "cheap" used; it prefers "inexpensive." And why wouldn't it push the more expensive wines? It makes more money on them, and that is why it is in business. But we say, forget the idea that you have to spend a lot of money to get a good-tasting wine.

Of course, we don't want you to misunderstand. We are not saying that the cheapest wine is the best wine for all occasions, because it certainly is not. But there are two very good reasons for beginning your wine education with the least expensive wines. The first is that this will give you a basis for comparison as your wine palate develops; and make no mistake about it, it will develop. The second reason is that often— not always, but often—the only difference between cheap and expensive wines is the length of aging time allowed for each.

We will have more to say later about

developing your wine palate, or taste for wine, if Making a Start you prefer. For now we simply want to point out to you that your tastes will change. And in fact, wines will change. The result is that what you like today you may not like next year, and conversely, the wine you do not like now might become one of your favorites within the next few months. But the only way you will have of comparing wines and making judgments about them is to know what the cheaper wines taste like.

To explain the second reason for starting with cheap wines, that often the only difference between cheap wines and expensive ones is the amount of aging given to each, we need to explain briefly how wine is made. It is not a mysterious process, no matter what you may have heard, and it can be very simple if done on a small scale, though admittedly commercial winemaking is quite a sophisticated process (see the eighth chapter, "Blending & Making Your Own Wine").

There really is not much more you can do to a bunch of grapes except crush them, put them in a barrel, and allow nature to take its course. What happens is that about seven days later you have a barrel of wine on your hands. And this is the point at which the character of this particular variety of wine is determined, first by the length of time the wine is aged, and second by the care with which the winery handles it. We are satisfied that most wineries treat their wines as gently as possible, but the matter of aging is a different story.

Wine is aged so it will be palatable. It is that simple. The process of aging changes the wine, softening and mellowing its tannins and acids.

Long ago the winemakers discovered that by removing the skins and stems from the barrel soon after the fermenting process had taken place, they could help the wine to age faster because tannins and acids were being eliminated. They also found that some wines age faster than others, and that by blending fast-aging wines with slow-aging ones they could produce a palatable wine in a shorter period of time.

In addition, the tremendous increase in demand for wine in this country has encouraged wineries to get their products into the stores in the shortest time possible. The result is that very few wineries age their wines any more than the absolute minimum that will give them a decent taste. And here we are talking about all wines, both cheap and expensive.

In fact, at a recent wine industry conference, one well-known winery explained that in order to age its wines properly, it would have to stop delivering its product to the stores for a period of two to three years. No company can afford to go without sales for that length of time without going into bankruptcy, so you can see for yourself that we consumers are being offered a lot of relatively unaged wine.

So these are the reasons why we say, find a cheap wine that suits your taste and enjoy it. You will not be far removed in taste from a wine that costs twice as much, you will be learning a basis for comparison and developing your wine palate, and you will not be wasting your money.

Incidentally, this may be the appropriate spot to lay to rest one of the old saws about cheap wine—that it will give you a worse hangover than will expensive wine. That is nonsense. **6** Cheap wine imbibed in the same amount as expensive wine will not give you a worse hangover. Overindulgence in *any* wine will cause a hangover, just as will overindulgence in any alcoholic beverage. It is how much wine you drink that determines how you will feel that next morning, not the price.

By now you have probably made a decision about this book. You have decided that we seem to be making sense; or you have decided that we are loonies and you are going to read on strictly for laughs. Either way, we are going to make a statement now that will probably cause cardiac arrest among the wine snobs.

Do not buy any imported wines, at least for a while. We urge you, as a beginning wine drinker, to stick to domestic wines from California and New York.

Why do we say that when "everyone knows" that the wines from France are superior to all others? Simply because they are not. That is another one of the fairy tales fostered and supported by the wine snobs. There are plenty of good, inexpensive wines produced in this country, especially in California, and it is much easier to make sense of them than of the imported wines. Many of them are also gaining worldwide recognition.

In addition, there is hardly such a thing as a bad California wine or a bad New York State wine. We do not mean that you will fall head over heels in love with every one you taste, because you won't. There will be some you like, some that are only tolerable, and some you will hate. But for the ones you don't like, you can be fairly sure it is not because they are bad wines. It is rather a case of "different strokes for different folks."

We cannot make that statement for foreign wines for two reasons. First, the climate in the United States in those areas that produce wine, and especially in California, is pretty much the same year after year, with the result that the winemakers know almost precisely what flavor, body, and bouquet their vineyards will produce —every year! But this is not true of most foreign wine-growing areas, where the vagaries of the weather can so affect a grape that it will be choice one year and simply awful the next. And of course, that is what "vintage year" is all about when it is applied to foreign wines, for the term refers to years when the weather permitted the grape to mature to near perfection. In California, on the other hand, the grape almost always matures in the same way from year to year, and the wines are almost always the same from year to year.

The second reason to stick with our domestic wines has to do with something we mentioned before, but only in passing: care in handling. Because wine is a living thing, actually alive and aging in the bottle, the way it is handled has quite a bit to do with the determination of its ultimate character.

Gentle handling and maintaining a constant temperature are highly desirable, in fact absolutely necessary, if wine is to be palatable when you open the bottle and take a sip. Foreign wines generally arrive in this country in the holds of cargo ships, which run hot and cold, and which shake, rattle, and roll around for perhaps weeks before arriving in port. What this does to a bottle of wine borders on criminal negligence.

8 Our domestic wines don't have to face such

brutal treatment, nor such drastic changes in temperature, and they are much better off.

As a little aside, we might mention that an acquaintance who was in the wine-importing business is convinced that much of the wine that comes into this country from foreign shores is the *worst* they have to offer, not the best, and far from the premium wine they claim it to be. We can only add that our own tastes seem to confirm her opinion, especially in the area of inexpensive wines.

Imported wine takes quite a beating on the high seas

These, then, are the reasons we urge you to stick with our domestically produced wines at **9**

first. Later, when you have become a lot more knowledgeable, when your wine palate has become more refined, you can—and should—take the plunge into buying foreign wines.

Before we get to the object of all this, which is to give you enough information so you can buy yourself a bottle of wine that will please you, we have a few notions about *where* you should buy wine. Do not, under any circumstances, just walk into any old store that sells wine and plunk down your money. Choose your wine store with care.

The first thing you want to look for is variety. We would say you want to have as wide a selection as possible. But don't interpret this to mean that the biggest is necessarily the best. There are other considerations.

You should note the care with which the wine is stored. Are the bottles with corks tilted so the cork will remain wet? If not, the cork can dry out, thus allowing air to enter the bottle, and the wine may be destroyed. Does it look like the wines are subjected to fluctuating temperatures? If it does, you should not buy your wine from this store because temperature change is one of the great enemies of wine and will cause it to spoil faster than you would think possible.

What about the well-known business principle called "turnover"? If the turnover is slow, the wine merchant had better be storing his wine properly or he is going to have shelves full of inferior wines. This problem is of little concern if you shop in the wine department of a supermarket because its turnover is usually rather rapid, but it will pay you to keep a watchful eye in any case.

10   A few months ago a customer asked us if

the Gallo Winery made two different types of Rhine wine. We said it did not. She went on to explain why she was asking. She had asked a dinner guest to pick up a bottle of Gallo Rhine wine on his way, and had specified that particular wine because she knew it would go well with what she was serving; she also knew she had half a bottle of it in her refrigerator. They began dinner with her half-bottle, and when that was finished they brought out the bottle just purchased by the guest. They were surprised to see that the second bottle had a different label than the first, and they were even more surprised when the second bottle turned out to be undrinkable. The wine was spoiled, and this almost spoiled the dinner.

A little detective work revealed that the bottle of wine had been purchased in an out-of-the-way grocery store that sold hardly any wine. The guest had gotten hold of a bottle of wine so old, in fact, that the label design had been changed not only once, but twice, since his wine had been bottled.

When you understand that white wines should be drunk relatively young, and that many merchants do not store their wine stock properly, you can see why we feel a rapid stock turnover is rather important. On the other hand, some of the smaller wine shops in those out-of-the-way places, whose turnover is admittedly slow, can prove to be veritable gold mines. It all depends upon whether or not the merchant has taken good care of his stock. If he has, you can occasionally pick up some great old wines that simply are not available elsewhere.

What about personal advice from the **11**

merchant himself? Great, if he knows what he is talking about, though few of them do. But if you are lucky you will find one who is both knowledgeable and courteous, someone who will spend enough time with you to make certain you get a wine that is close to what you are looking for.

Rest assured that the profit picture for the wine merchant is such that he can well afford to give you a few minutes to help you make a choice. If he won't, take your business elsewhere, for all he is interested in is making a profit, not in satisfying his customers. On the other hand, you should not make a nuisance of yourself. People are in business to make money.

Need we warn you against asking the boxboy what wine you should buy? We hope not.

So! Now you have looked at a number of stores and chosen the one where you want to buy some wine. You walk through the door, and immediately you are confronted with such a variety of bottles and labels that all your original confusion returns and you feel like giving up. Don't do it; forge right ahead.

When you look at the label on any bottle of wine, you may be under the impression that it will tell you all you need to know in order to make a selection. Don't kid yourself. It does not matter how long you browse about reading all the different wine labels— you simply will not be able to tell what is inside a bottle of wine until you open it and give it the taste test. We explain how to read a wine label in the third chapter, so we will **12** not go into that now, but for the present believe us when we say that it does not tell you very much.

So in the beginning there are only two things you need to have in mind when you walk into that store you have carefully selected. You should know what you want the wine for, which is to say you will know whether you are looking for an everyday table wine or a peace-offering wine to go with the stuffed salmon your mother-in-law is preparing. And, naturally, you will know what each particular wine is like, having read the sections of this book that describe this as well as words can.

From this point on the key word for you to remember is *flexibility*. You absolutely must make up your mind that you are going to be flexible in your enjoyment of wine. We have an acquaintance who turns up her nose at every wine she tastes except dry whites. One sip of a medium-dry white wine and she climbs onto her soapbox and gives you fifteen minutes on what a lousy wine it is. Not only is this the height of wine snobbery, it is bad-mannered foolishness besides.

We can honestly say that, barring those that have spoiled, we have never tasted a wine we did not enjoy in some way or other. That is a pretty strong statement, and we do not mean to say that we have not been disappointed, because we have. What we mean is that we have attempted to train ourselves to accept each wine for *what it is*, not for what we expect it to be. And if we *are* disappointed we simply try to forget what we anticipated from that particular wine, so that we can enjoy it for what it actually is. **13**

This is the attitude we urge you to adopt. Be flexible, open, and inquiring. It is *not* one of the Ten Commandments of Wine that all white wines have to be dry. So if you sample a wine and expect a dry white but find that you have bought a sweeter medium-dry instead, put aside any disappointment and enjoy your purchase for what it is. At the very least you have added to your knowledge of wine. At best, you have discovered a brand-new favorite.

Developing Your Tastes

Wine divides very neatly into three categories according to its color—red, white, and rosé. We will discuss each of these types of wine in this chapter, but first we want to say a few words about your wine palate, with the emphasis on "your."

You will discover fairly quickly that you already have definite likes and dislikes among the wines you taste. But if we may take the liberty of repeating ourselves, your tastes will change as time goes by. So do not be afraid to try a second time a wine that you once did not like.

Let us again caution you against the idea that you have to spend a lot of money to get a good-tasting wine. You don't. The wine industry has done such a good selling job on the American public that most people are convinced they have to pay a lot to get a good wine. Actually, we believe there is not a bottle of wine going that is worth more than $10. And that is for red wine. For white wine you can cut our top limit in half, to about $5. There are some exceptions, but they are quite rare.

We have spent more than our limit for a 15

bottle of wine a few times, but it was done only out of curiosity and we have yet to be convinced we got our money's worth. Which leads us to the question, how much better is the best over the worst? The only answer we can give is that it is strictly a matter of taste. It is really nonsense to talk about one wine as a "quality" wine and another as not. While there may be a general consensus that one wine is better than another, what you are really talking about is individual taste preference. To be a little more specific, if you like a jug wine (a term we use to denote wine sold in any quantity larger than a fifth) that costs around $3 a gallon, such as Cribari Burgundy, it is silly to think that another Burgundy selling for $4 a *half-gallon* will necessarily be better. One of the two may suit your taste better, but we guarantee that it will not be the price that makes the difference. It will be your wine palate.

How refined can you expect your own palate to become? You will certainly be surprised. You will not become an expert overnight, but a year from now we think you will be able to make good selections without much trouble. Actually, most people—including many so-called experts—are unable to distinguish between two wines that are fairly close in taste and body, whatever their expertise.

An incident of mislabeling might help convince you of this. Early in 1974 the *Los Angeles Times* reported that the Almadén Winery had been fined by the federal government and suspended from marketing for a period of three weeks in California by that

state's Alcoholic Beverage Control Department for allegedly mislabeling one of its wines. The wine in question was being labeled as a varietal wine, which means that by state law it had to contain a minimum of 51 percent of the particular variety of grape for which it was named. According to the Alcoholic Beverage Control Department, Almadén was not maintaining that percentage and was therefore in violation of the law.

Without unfairly accusing Almadén and without being vindictive, we can say that there is almost no way a consumer could tell how long the mislabeling had been going on, or even whether other wineries are guilty of the same error and Almadén was the one unfortunate enough to get caught. Perhaps this is an isolated case; perhaps not. Our point is this: that not one out of a hundred thousand consumers has a wine palate developed to the extent that he could catch such a mislabeling incident.

This is probably the best place to point out that no matter how well your palate develops, certain things will affect it adversely. You have heard, we suppose, the old expression, "off your feed." When you have a head cold, for example, food just does not taste right to you. The same is true where wine is concerned. Your wine palate can be off because of a cold or another illness.

Another thing that will throw your wine palate out of kilter is hard liquor. Too many cocktails or highballs before dinner will absolutely destroy your wine palate, making it impossible for your to distinguish any gradations of taste. If you have ever wondered why many of the better restaurants do not serve **17** liquor, there is your answer—because they know what it will do to your enjoyment of their fine food and wine. And when you are paying $15, $20, or more for a dinner, you really should be able to appreciate it. Likewise, too much tobacco will deaden your palate and affect the taste of the wine you want to drink. So any time you are going to use your wine palate, treat it gently beforehand.

We now want to tell you how wines are named. We mentioned the word "varietal" before, and we want to define the word, and its counterpart, "generic," because most wines are named in one of these ways.

Varietal refers to a wine named after a variety of grape. According to California law, as pointed out above, if a winery is going to label a wine by the name of a grape, the wine must contain at least 51 percent of that particular grape. The wine could, and often does, have a greater percentage than that, but 51 percent is the minimum. A Cabernet Sauvignon is an example of a varietal wine, as are Pinot Chardonnay and Zinfandel.

A generically named wine, on the other hand, is not named after a grape, but rather usually after one of the wine-growing regions of Europe. Burgundy is a rather common example. There is no such thing as a Burgundy grape, but we all know about Burgundy wine. Do not get the idea, however, that all Burgundy wines come from the French region of Burgundy, because they do not. California produces some of the world's finest Burgundies. Simply remember that a generic label, such as Burgundy, refers to a type of wine and not a particular grape. Other examples of generic wine names are Chablis and Moselle.

There is a third way in which wines are named. A winery can simply make up a name for a wine—this is called a proprietary name. Examples of this are Paul Masson "Emerald Dry," and Christian Brothers "Château Lasalle." This is the least desirable way to designate wines, in our opinion, because the consumer has no frame of reference for the name. But it is done by some wineries, and we have to live with it.

In any discussion of wine, quite a large number of descriptive terms are used, and we would like to explain some of them. Let us warn you, however, that because they are all relative terms, considerable confusion can arise. We will try to be as clear as we can, but remember that despite the terminology your own palate must ultimately be the judge of what the terms mean to you.

There are two terms that mean different things on opposite sides of the ocean, and we might as well get them out of the way first. The first term is the French word *haut*, pronounced "oh." In France the word means "high," and when applied to wine generally means "dry." Strangely, the word has come to mean "sweet" in this country. Similarly, the French word *sec* also means "dry" in France and "sweet" in the United States. We do not know why there is this confusion of meanings, but it is important for you to sort it out and try to remember which is which.

Fruity. If a wine has a fruity taste it means that you can taste the grape from which the wine was made. A wine is not **19** fruity if you cannot taste the grape. It is as simple as that.

Chewy. We are not sure whether we made up this term or whether it just is not used much, but it really does not matter. This is basically a red wine term, and it means that you are left with something in your mouth after you take a drink. It has to do with substance, and is similar to the words "heavy" and "full-bodied." Perhaps the best way to explain it is to use an analogy. You are probably aware that many of the cake mixes advertised in the media are praised as being "light." Well, nothing turns us off faster than a light cake. We like to know we are eating something, which is to say we like "chewy" cakes. So, if you can follow our analogy, a chewy wine will not disappear as soon as you put it in your mouth; it has substance and it will stay with you for a while, almost to the extent that you can use your upper and lower molars on it.

Full-bodied. This term means that the wine so described is essentially balanced, that no one particular characteristic sticks out. If you put too much salt in one of your cakes, the salty taste will stand out. But if you have a perfect blend of ingredients in the cake it will be full-bodied, just as a well-balanced wine will be full-bodied. *Well-rounded,* another frequently used term, means pretty much the same thing.

Musty. The word "musty" does not sound good perhaps, but it certainly fits some wines. If you drink a wine and the taste reminds you of cobwebs in the wine cellar of a forgotten monastery, you have experienced a musty wine. Usually a musty wine will smell like a dark cool cellar. It is very similar to earthy, but perhaps a bit more extreme, and can be very good.

Zestful. This is a fairly straightforward term that is self-explanatory. It means lively and light. One way in which we use this term is to describe some of our favorite Champagnes, those which tickle the nose and may even bring a tear to the eye, as opposed to those which have a heavy bitterness about them and which we do not particularly care for.

Velvety. When you experience a soft and smooth quality about a wine, it is velvety. There definitely is not any harshness present.

Mellow. To us the word "mellow" should be reserved exclusively for those wines which have been fully aged. One sip of an eight-year-old Cabernet Sauvignon, followed by a sip of a two-year-old wine of the same variety, will demonstrate the difference and quickly tell you what the "mellow" means.

Dry. One of the most common terms used in describing certain wines, this is easily misunderstood by the beginner. "Dry" means an absence of sweetness, but it certainly does not mean "sour." The hyphenated terms "semi-dry" and "medium-dry" are mere taste-value judgments made by wineries and wine tasters, and you must determine what they mean by your own taste test. The word "dry" is additionally used to distinguish table wines of 14 percent or less alcoholic content from "sweet" or "dessert" wines with an alcoholic content in the vicinity of 20 percent.

Brut. When we use this term we restrict **21**

it to sparkling wines, those with effervescence. It means they are dry, but you will soon discover that brut Champagnes quite frequently have a touch of sweetness about them, so be prepared for it.

There are dozens of other terms that are used to describe the various characteristics of wines, but we do not believe it is necessary to try to define them all, for so much of their meaning depends upon the opinion of the person using them. Such terms will make much more sense to you when you taste a wine and have a particular taste sensation to tie them to. Thus, we leave it at that.

As you read further along in the book you will notice that most of the examples we use will be California wines, rather than imported ones. We have done this because we firmly believe, as we have said before, that beginning wine drinkers should start with domestic wines, and of these California's are the most widely available. Those of you who live in a major marketing area of the country will not have any trouble locating imported wines, but not all of us reside in such areas, and not all of us have a well-stocked wine store around the corner. But almost anyone in this country has access to a decent selection of California wines.

Later on, of course, as your palate develops and you want to learn about French, German and Italian wines, much of the same information will apply. But by then you will be aware, we hope, that California wines and imported wines are not truly comparable. Can you, for example, compare white cake with chocolate cake? Both can be good cakes, certainly, but not of the same kind. It is possible, on the other hand, to compare two different chocolate cakes to determine which you like better, for both are of one kind.

Thus, we believe that comparing California wines with imported wines is unfair to both. To declare, as many wine snobs do, that all French wines are superior to all California wines is foolish, just as the reverse declaration would be, that all California wines are superior. It all depends upon what you like to taste, and tastes certainly do differ.

This wide difference in taste between wines from different countries, even though they may be of the same variety, is easily explained. Because the type of soil in which the grape is grown has almost everything to do with the basic taste of that grape, two different soils will produce two different tastes from the same variety of grape. The sugar content of the grape, its acid and tannin content, and the handling of the wine made from that grape all combine to affect its taste. You might, for example, enjoy both a Napa Valley Burgundy and a French Burgundy, but the tastes will be much different; both good, but different.

Incidentally, it might interest you to know that the very poorest of soil produces the very finest of wines. You might think that the Mississippi River delta country would be a great place to grow wine grapes because of its fertile soil, but it is not. The soil is too rich, and the grape picks up too much earthiness; neither will the grape pick up the acids and tannins it needs from overly rich soils.

This "earthiness" we refer to is charac-   **23**

teristic of French wines, and has to do with the taste imparted to the grape from the makeup of the soil. That is not to say, obviously, that French wines taste like dirt. It is simply an attempt to describe a certain taste picked up from the growing medium, in this case the soil. A similar earthiness is present in many of the New York State wines from the Finger Lakes region. There are some very fine New York State wines, and they are more like French wines in character than are California wines.

While we are touching briefly on the subject of French wines, we should say a word or two about the French *vin ordinaire*. How many times have you heard someone returning from a trip to France rave about the quality of the cheap, everyday variety of French wine that they bought in a small country village? Or, better yet, perhaps you have experienced it yourself.

We believe that this *vin ordinaire* is superior to most of the wines sent over here by the French because it simply has not been juggled around in cargo ships, beaten up by dock hands, or subjected to the extremes of heat and cold that occur on a long ocean voyage. Actually, *vin ordinaire* is nothing more or less than the French counterpart of our cheaper domestic wines—Italian Swiss Colony Zinfandel or Paul Masson Chablis, to give you two examples. This is another case in which so-called wine experts have tried to brainwash us through their advertising into thinking wine has to be expensive to be good. Taste some of California's "ordinary wine" and we feel sure you will agree with us.

Now let us talk about the wines themselves, first discussing red wines, then whites, and finally rosés. We will mention many types and varieties, some more common than others. We urge you to first concentrate on the common varieties, and only later move into those that are not so well known.

And we warn you at the start that for almost every generalization we make, there will be an exception. Sorry, but that is the way it is with wine. So we suggest you try to get an overall picture first, and then go back and read for detail. That way you will be able to see where the exceptions fit in and can—we hope—make sense of the entire subject.

Red Wine

Red wines get their color from pigments that are in the grapes and grape skins, and therefore the longer the skins are left in the fermenting mixture, the darker and redder the color of the wine from a particular variety of grape will be. The skin of the grape also imparts most of the tannins and acids to the wine.

The most common red wine, probably the most common wine of any kind is Burgundy. "Burgundy" is one of the generic names, and anything called Burgundy will be a blend of wines made from different grapes; which grapes in what amounts depends upon the winery. The most commonly used grapes are the Zinfandel, the Petite Sirah, and the Carignane. If the wine is made only from these varieties it will be a light blend; for

25

heaviness and a fuller body the Barberra is used, as are the Cabernet Sauvignon and the Pinot Noir.

A second common red wine is Claret, again a generic type. Claret is an English term that was originally applied to red wines from the French region of Bordeaux. Today it generally means a red wine that is lighter in both body and color than the Burgundies, and reminiscent of Bordeaux red wines. The Cabernet Sauvignon grape is widely used to make Clarets.

It is an absolute rule that one winery's version of Burgundy will taste quite different from another's, and the same rule holds true for Clarets. The reason is simply that the different grapes used are blended in varying proportions to make the wine. One winery may use 20 percent Cabernet Sauvignon in its blend, while another just down the road might use as much as 40 percent. Both wineries are producing a generic red wine, but the tastes will be different. It is, therefore, a corollary to this rule that you cannot tell what a generic Burgundy or Claret will taste like until you open a bottle and sample it. These red generics are the wines we suggest you start with, sampling a number of them until you find one or two that you particularly like.

The varietal red wine from California that has the best reputation is Cabernet Sauvignon (Claret-type), followed closely by Pinot Noir (Burgundy-type). The Cabernet Sauvignon is exceptionally smooth in its better versions, fruity in taste, and heavy-bodied. The Pinot Noir should be rich and robust, generally astringent because the skins are left in the fermenting mixture longer than with most other red wines, and also fairly heavy.

Major wine-producing areas in California:

1. Sonoma/Mendocino
2. Napa
3. Lodi
4. Livermore
5. Fresno/San Joaquin
6. Cucamonga/Los Angeles
7. Fallbrook

Zinfandel is another varietal red wine. It used to have the connotation of being the wine drunk by winos, but today it is fully accepted as a good everyday wine. In our opinion it is difficult to surpass a nice Zinfandel for that use. You will also be seeing

27

more and more Ruby Cabernet in the future,
a varietal made from a grape developed by the
University of California at Davis, crossing the
Cabernet Sauvignon with the Carignane.

The well-known Chianti wine is a generic,
and whether it is from California or Italy, it
should be dry, medium-bodied, and have a
strong flavor.

Taylor's Lake Country Red, from New
York State, is one of the proprietary-named
wines, and it is somewhat more astringent
than most California red wines. Bully Hill
wines from New York are less widely known,
but where available they provide the consumer
with fantastic buys in generic reds.

As far as age of red wines is concerned,
this is a "mixed bag." Harry Waugh, one of
the few wine-expert/writers who never tries to
fool his readers, claims that "it's a common
fallacy to think that the older a red wine is,
the better it will be." We will go deeper into
this subject in later chapters, but for now let
us say that we agree with the notion that
modern red Burgundies, and even some of the
red wines from Bordeaux, will not keep as
long as they used to. Furthermore, Zinfandels
will be quite acceptable after only a year.
There are exceptions, but as a general rule
there are very few wines that *gain* from
having more than five or six years of aging.
Many will hold their peak longer than that,
but few will improve.

French red wines are almost always
named for a geographical area, a subject we
consider in more detail in the third chapter,
"Reading a Wine Label." For now we will
28 try to describe some of these wines.

From the Bordeaux region, the best-known red wines are from Medoc, St.-Emilion, and Pomerol. A Medoc is fairly dry and medium-bodied. St.-Emilion wines are full-bodied and robust, again with a dry finish, while those from Pomerol are a bit lighter.

The best-known French Burgundies are those from the Côte-d'Or region, which includes the townships of Nuits-St.-Georges and Pommard. We enjoy the Pommard, which is fruity and full-bodied, but only when it has been aged about ten years, for then it is soft and velvety. Our favorite, however, is the Nuits-St.-Georges, which is beautifully balanced and soft, and which leaves you with a delightful aftertaste.

Another region, the Côtes-du-Rhône, also produces red wines which are full-bodied and vigorous. The outstanding example is the wine from Châteauneuf-du-Pape, which is velvety-rich and round, and is available most of the time.

In a separate category are the red wines from southern Burgundy, the best-known of which are those from Beaujolais. French Beaujolais wines are favorites of ours, mainly because they are refreshing and light-bodied without being innocuous. It is a basic premise that they must be consumed young, however, because they do not contain enough tannins and acids to give them a long life span. By young we mean within two or three years of their vintage. These wines are produced primarily from the Gamay grape, which enjoys wide use in California also, but do not think that a varietal Gamay or Gamay Beaujolais from California will be similar to

29

the French Beaujolais; the former lack the earthy flavor of the French wines.

Italian red wines are led in popularity by Chianti, and Chianti Classico is one of the better versions. A Chianti Riserva will generally be fuller-bodied, but also more expensive. Valpolicella is fruitier and more fragrant, with a velvet edge. Bardolino wine is lighter and fresher, and most people like to drink it at a relatively young age. Lambrusco can be either a red or a white wine. It is light and fairly sweet, and it will froth when poured into the glass; it is bubbly, but not as much as Champagne. It reminds us more of Spanish Sangria than anything else.

Now we are not embarrassed to admit that there are hundreds of red wines we have not mentioned. We have not overlooked them, nor have we eliminated them because they are inferior. We have stayed with the better-known versions because they are what you, the beginning wine drinker, will build your wine-knowledge foundation upon, and they are the ones you will come across most frequently.

Again we urge you to begin with the inexpensive versions and work your way up. Blind taste tests have proven that even many of the so-called experts cannot tell the difference between a decently aged Claret and a blended Cabernet Sauvignon, and the former is quite a bit cheaper. There is, naturally, a distinct difference between a ten-year-old Cabernet Sauvignon and a one-year-old Claret, but anyone could tell this at the first sip. So trust yourself and your own wine palate, and do not be too impressed with obscure and expensive wines. That way you will really appreciate the finer wines you will eventually buy, and will not be deluded by high prices without comparable value.

White Wine

Approximately 95 percent of all white wines are produced, quite naturally, from white grapes. Under most circumstances, when the grapes are pressed to release the juice, quite a bit of care is taken to avoid crushing the seed, because broken seeds will impart an undesirable bitterness to the wine. Because lighter, livelier white wines are better sellers than heavy ones, most wineries do not allow the skins to remain too long in the fermenting mixture.

One of the exceptions to this generalization is the Pinot Noir grape, which has a blue-black skin but a white juice. When this grape is fermented with its skin it produces the famed red wine, Pinot Noir. But when fermented without its skin the juice makes white wine, which in turn is used to make some of the very finest of Champagnes.

The most common white wine is Chablis, a generic name taken from the Chablis township in the region of Burgundy. Because of the location in Burgundy the wine was for many years called "white Burgundy," but this designation has passed out of fashion in recent times. California winemakers produce quite a bit of Chablis, usually bottling a wine that is reasonably dry and fruity, and often selling it in gallons and half-gallons. In our opinion California Chablis is an excellent **31** everyday wine; the key, of course, is to try different brands until you find one you particularly enjoy. We find some versions of Chablis to be as good as many white varietals, yet much less expensive.

Another generic white wine that is fairly well-known is Rhine wine, which is usually a shade sweeter than Chablis. There are many Riesling wines, but they almost always have a slightly sweet taste. Generic Rieslings are blends of Riesling and Sylvaner grapes, and are to be distinguished from varietal Riesling wines such as the Johannisberg Riesling. Because generic Rhine and Riesling wines, along with Semillons, are so confusingly labeled, it is very difficult to know what to expect from any of them unless you have tasted them. All you can assume is that they will be slightly sweeter than Chablis.

Sauternes from California are a bit easier to sort out, although to do so you must not relate them to French Sauternes. In California, Sauterne and Dry Sauterne are invariably dry, and are practically interchangeable on that score with Chablis. On the other hand, Haut Sauternes are sweeter, but not as sweet as French Sauternes. Some wines that are labeled Sauterne are actually Semillons, will be so indicated by a subtitle, and will be dry and fragrant.

California white varietals are numerous. Probably the best known is the Pinot Chardonnay, produced from the Chardonnay grape of Chablis heritage; the good reputation is well-deserved. Pinot Chardonnary wines are dry, some of them the "driest," and usually full-flavored.

The wine Chenin Blanc is light and fresh, and sweeter than Pinot Chardonnay. Gewürztraminer and Traminer wines are often confused because of the similarity in names, but they are actually quite different. The Gewürztraminer has a spiciness that is quite unique; the Traminer, on the other hand, is light and fruity in its better versions.

The Johannisberg Riesling, mentioned above, is a varietal wine that is slightly sweet and dominantly fruity. It is highly regarded as a varietal, and should be distinguished from the generic Rieslings, which are generally made from altogether different grapes.

Where imported white wines are concerned, the beginning wine drinker seems to be familiar with the names of the wines, but not with the wines themselves. As was the case with red wines, a smattering of geographical knowledge is very helpful.

From Germany there are two broad classes of white wine, Rhine and Moselle. Under these two classes the wines are further delineated with the name of a village; for example, Piesporter and Bernkasteler from Moselle, and Rüdesheimer and Johannisberger from the Rhine. When these designations are combined with the rest of the information on the label (see the third chapter, "Reading a Wine Label"), a fairly accurate idea of the general characteristics of the wine is possible. It should be noted, however, that the village designations are not to be taken literally; that is, a Piesporter does not come entirely from that village, but rather from many unnamed villages and vineyards in the area.

In general you will find that Moselle

wines are light-bodied, slightly tart, and fresh.
Rhine wines are sweeter, softer, and have
more body. The Riesling grape is the one
generally planted along the Moselle River and
in the Rhine area around Johannisberg and
Rüdesheim. The Sylvaner grape is used to
produce some Liebfraumilch, but aside from
that wine, which varies in quality to a great
degree, you will probably find nothing special
about its use. If the word "Riesling" appears
on a label, it means that at least 75 percent of
the wine must be made from that variety of
grape.

When you begin to look for one or two
German wines to try, we think you will find it
easier if you stay with those that are imported
by reputable shippers. Incidentally, the finest
white wine we have tasted in years was a 1971
Moselle of high pedigree, and yet it was so
expensive we would not buy it again because
it was not *that* much better than versions of
the same that sell for much less. Buying from
a reputable shipper will allow you to get a
good wine at a reasonable cost, and there will
be at most only a slight difference from wines
that are priced much higher.

White wines from France are, perhaps, a
little more difficult to sort out, but again
geographical knowledge is quite helpful.

We have mentioned Chablis in connection
with California white wines, and we need only
add that French Chablis should be very dry
and light. A varietal version is Pinot Chardonnay. Better known, and now becoming the
favorite of many Americans, is Pouilly Fuissé
from southern Burgundy. We have mixed
34 feelings about this wine; often it is undis-

tinguished, overpriced, and varies greatly in quality, though admittedly in its better versions it is quite dry and delicate. A much better value, in our opinion, is the white wine from Puligny-Montrachet.

White Bordeaux wines include those from Sauternes, Graves, and Barsac. French Sauternes are always sweet and fruity, and Barsacs, from a township within Sauternes, are a shade drier but still sweet. There is no other wine quite like a Barsac, so you should sample it at some time or other. Wines from Graves are usually fresher and fruitier in comparison, and may be either dry or medium-dry. Sometimes the shippers will make up a special name for their white Bordeaux wines (Mouton-Cadet is a familiar example), and as with all proprietary names, care must be taken to know what you are buying.

The Loire River area produces some very nice white wines, but for some reason they are often overlooked and they do not have the reputation of other French whites. Muscadet wines, no relation to Muscatels, are dry, delicate, and fresh, and should be drunk as young as possible. Pouilly Fumé wines are earthy and perfumy, with a more distinct flavor. Perhaps one of the most underrated wines ever is that from Vouvray. It is a soft, medium-dry wine, and at its best is quite mellow and appealing.

Wines from the Alsace region of France are sold under varietal names, not geographical, and the most famous of them is Gewürztraminer. Gewürztraminer is the wine we said was spicy when we mentioned it in connection with California varietals, and the version from

Alsace is similar, perhaps with more body.
The wine is so distinct in taste that many
neophyte wine drinkers dislike it, but you
should try it, because there is no other wine
quite like it. California Gewürztraminers compare favorably in quality, in our opinion.

The best-known white wine from Italy is
Soave, made from a blend of Garganega and
Trebbiano grapes. Never as delicate as a fine
Chablis, a good Soave is well-balanced, fresh,
and fragrant.

This is the appropriate place to mention a
phenomenon known as *Botrytis cinerea,* sometimes called the "noble rot." It is a mold
that attacks the grapes, causing them to
wither, but concentrating their richness. Wine
made from grapes afflicted with the Botrytis
mold have an extremely delicate flavor that
will disappear with age, so they must be consumed young. The mold occurs much more
frequently in foreign countries than in the
United States, but in 1972 it was found in
certain areas of California. Such wines will
usually be labeled in some way that tells you
of the Botrytis phenomenon, perhaps by a
note on the back label, perhaps by the terms
"Spätlese" or "Auslese" (see the third chapter, "Reading a Wine Label").

As a general rule, white wines do not age
very well, and part of their charm is the fresh-
ness derived from their youth. Under controlled conditions white wines will stay, or
hold, for six to eight years, although in that
case you are "keeping" the wines, rather than
aging them for improvement, as you do with
red wines. At any rate, we follow the injunc-
tion, the newer the better.

No matter how little experience you have had
with wine, it is likely that somewhere along
the way you have tasted a Rosé wine. The
word "Rosé" on the label indicates nothing
more than the color of the wine; there is no
such thing as a Rosé grape. Some wineries,
indeed, simply call this kind of wine "pink
table wine."

The most popular of all Rosé wines in
this country is produced from the Grenache
grape, and is therefore labeled Grenache Rosé.
It is almost always noticeably sweet. Rosé
wines are also made from the Gamay grape.
In that case the skins are left in the fermenting mixture for only a short period of time,
less than two days, then removed, for if they
were left in any longer the wine would become Gamay Beaujolais, a light-bodied red
wine. We call both the Grenache Rosé and the
Gamay Rosé "true" Rosés.

Many, if not most, Rosés are not "true"
Rosés, because they are made by blending
together red and white wines. Some of these
are every bit as good as what we call "true"
Rosés, and they come in many shades and
hues of pink. The winemaster blends them for
both taste and color, and a high degree of
consistency is not unusual from year to year.
Finding one that suits your palate is merely a
matter of experimenting, for Rosés are available in a wide range of flavor, dryness, and
aroma.

Two particular areas of France produce
Rosé wines that are generally considered the
finest in the world. Tavel Rosés, from the Rhône   **37**

area near Chateauneuf-du-Pape, are usually dry. Anjou Rosés from the Loire River Valley are usually a touch sweeter. The most popular imported Rosé is undoubtedly Mateus from Portugal, a slightly sweet version. We feel that because Rosés are such undistinguished wines at best, the imports are all overpriced and we rarely buy them.

The sweetest of all Rosés are those produced in New York State, notably Taylor's Lake Country Pink and Gold Seal's Catawba Pink. If you find that you prefer sweeter Rosés, there is certainly no reason to spend any extra money for the imports when New York Rosés are so well made. To do so would simply be another demonstration of wine snobbery.

No amount of verbal or written description can substitute for the actual experience of tasting a wine, whether it be red, white, or pink. We have tried to help you by giving generalizations, but these by themselves are not enough for you to tell whether or not you will be pleased by a certain wine. However, after you taste a few of these wines, a second reading of this chapter may put the information we have given into a different frame of reference, one tied closely enough to your own experience that it will be more helpful.

Reading a Wine Label

Remember the proverb, "You can't judge a book by its cover"? Keep it in mind as you read this chapter, for if ever an old saying was applicable, this is the time. Certainly wine labels do tell you something about what is inside the bottle, just as book covers tell you the title of the book and the author's name; but just as you cannot judge the quality of the text by the cover of the book, so you can not tell what a wine will taste like merely by reading its label.

Generally the federal and state laws that cover wine labeling require that certain items of information be included on every bottle. The information is: (1) the quantity, if this is not molded into the glass of the bottle; (2) the alcoholic content of the wine; (3) where the wine comes from; (4) who makes the wine. No matter where the wine was produced, whether in California, New York, Germany, or France, at least the above information will be printed on the label. And this is enough information for you to get a general idea about a bottle of wine, but not anything too specific.

The first two items are fairly straight- 39

forward. Usually the quantity of the bottle will be listed as a fifth, a quart, a half-gallon, or a gallon. The fifth is called that because it is one-fifth of a gallon (which also makes it four-fifths of a quart), and is what we refer to when we mention a "bottle" of wine. Half-gallons and gallons we call "jugs" of wine. Magnums and jeroboams are bottle sizes generally used for Champagnes; a magnum is a bit more than a quart and a half, a jeroboam a little more than three quarts.

Certain imported wines are measured in liters, and in line with the movement in the United States to convert to the metric system, proposals have been made to change wine bottle standards so they, too, will be measured in metrics. Such a change could happen very soon, perhaps as early as 1977. The following table lists the metric sizes with their present counterparts:

Metric	*Present size*
¾ liter	fifth
1 liter	quart
1½ liters	magnum
3 liters	jeroboam

The most common sizes will be, of course, the ¾ liter (comparable to the fifth) and the 1 liter (comparable to the quart). A liter actually equals 1.0567 quarts; to put it another way, while a quart is 32 ounces, a liter is 33.814 ounces. Not very much difference, as you can see, but if the proposals are adopted you should know what a liter represents.

40   The alcoholic content of a wine determines whether that wine is a "table" wine or a "dessert" wine. Simply put, table wine can contain no more than 14 percent alcohol, though it may contain less. If a wine has more than that percentage of alcohol in it, it is called dessert wine (a subject we discuss in the chapter on appetizer and dessert wines). But it is important for you to understand why the limit is 14 percent, because it has to do with the way alcohol gets into the wine.

It begins with Mother Nature. The white powder you see on the skin of a grape is natural yeast. When the grape is crushed to begin the winemaking process, this yeast comes into contact with the natural sugar inside the grape. The sugar then begins to ferment. As long as any sugar remains in the mixture, the yeast keeps on working. When the sugar is completely used up, so to speak, the yeast stops its action and the fermentation is complete.

Because all the sugar is "used up," the wine so made is as dry as that particular grape can make, and owing to the combination of ingredients (yeast and sugar) placed in and on the grape by nature, the wine simply cannot have an alcoholic content over 14 percent. It may be less, according to the grapes that are used, but it cannot be more.

But suppose the winemaker does not want a dry wine, but wants a wine with a sweet finish. He stops the fermentation at an earlier point by adding enough grape brandy —otherwise known as alcohol—to bring the wine's alcoholic content up to the 14 percent limit. The mixture, having reached Mother Nature's limit, stops fermenting, and the **41** resulting unfermented sugar residue gives the wine the sweet finish that the winemaker desired.

What happens if the winemaker puts more than 14 percent alcohol into the wine? He has, very simply, made a dessert wine, in which the wineries usually strive for a 20 percent alcoholic content. That is, when the mix reaches the 14 percent alcoholic content level and stops fermenting, as it always will, the winemaker adds the additional alcohol. This gives dessert wines more body, a different character, guarantees their stability, and allows you to keep them longer.

Considering all this, it is fairly clear that the only information you get from knowing the alcoholic content of a wine is that it is either a table wine or a dessert wine, one or the other (remembering, of course, that there are exceptions, notably in fruit wines).

The rest of the information on a wine label is certainly more interesting, and it can

California labels: *a*, generic; *b*, varietal

Key to labels:

1. Alcoholic content
2. Contents
3. Brand name—producer or importer
4. Type of wine

a

b

be more informative. For many people, looking for good but little-known wines is an adventure, comparable to browsing for a rare book or shopping for an antique. There is a certain measure of pride in making a "find." And there is little doubt that as you learn to read and understand a wine label, much of the trial-and-error aspect is eliminated and you can begin to recognize the kinds of wines that you enjoy. But bear in mind that it is still a gamble to choose a wine solely by its label, if you have never tasted that wine before. We are not saying you should not or that it can't be fun, just that it is a gamble.

Before we go any further, a word of warning is in order. Please do not be deluded into thinking that a wine will be good just because the label has been printed in a handsome design. It may seem obvious, but it is true—beauty is only skin deep. And a beautiful wine label is absolutely no guarantee of a beautiful wine.

Reading a Wine Label

Key to labels (cont.):

5. Vintage
6. Meaningless terms and phrases
7. Regulating agency

Imported labels: *a*, generic; *b*, specific

Reading
a Wine Label

The technique for reading wine labels and learning from them is to be aware of certain key words. The two most important items to look for on the label are where the wine comes from and who makes it. Important to a lesser degree is the vintage of the wine.

Our method of surveying a wine label is to first look for the place of origin. In could be listed as a country, a state, a county, a district, or even something more specific. And the more precise this information is, the better you will be able to judge what it is you are looking at.

The most specific a wine label can be is to name a vineyard or a certain plot of ground on which the grapes were grown, but this is rather unusual. It is more common to see something less specific.

Let us take the word "Napa" as an example, for it is quite well-known. Seeing "Napa" on the label tells you that the wine came from the Napa Valley in northern California. This is a fairly small area geographically, but one that is highly respected for its wine-grape growing suitability. If "Napa" is the only designation, the chances are that the wine is a blend made from grapes grown in a number of different vineyards, and that all the vineyards are located in the Napa Valley.

An even more specific designation is the phrase, "Estate Bottled." This generally means that the grapes used to make the wine in question were grown on the property of the winery—on the winery's "estate." It used to be that wineries reserved this term for the best **44** wine they had to offer. This is *not necessarily* true today, owing—no doubt—to the demand for high production volume, but you will still find some wineries that maintain the integrity of the term.

The comparable French term to "Estate Bottled" is "Château." Probably the most famous chateau bottling in history is Château Lafite-Rothschild; other well-known ones are Château Latour, Château Chambertain, and Château Montrachet. Château bottling has a slightly different meaning than estate bottling, in that it means the wine was made and bottled on the château, but not that the grapes were grown there. In France the term "produced by" means that the château grew the grapes.

Incidentally, with very few exceptions, a single variety of grape from a single vineyard does not make a good wine. Several different varieties from the same vineyard do.

But once again caution is in order. The labeling of a wine as "Estate Bottled" or "Château Bottled" does not guarantee that the wine will be outstanding. This is our old "book by the cover" warning again. Simply because some grapes were grown on a specified plot of ground, you cannot assume that they will have made an exceptional wine. They may have, but they also may *not* have. So do not go head over heels after a wine just because it is estate bottled. Taste-test a bottle first.

Let us take an example from France next. In Bordeaux there is an area called St.-Emilion, and a village in that district called St.-Georges. A farmer (grape grower) in that village might produce his own wine from the **45** best of the grapes that he grows, and that wine will be labeled with that farmer's name (his château) or his village. The same farmer will sell the rest of his grape crop, probably a little less than his best, to a bulk wine producer in his area, and this wine will be labeled St.-Emilion. If the farmer sells his grapes to a wine producer outside the area of St.-Emilion, who blends them with grapes from other areas, the wine produced would be called simply Bordeaux.

So generally speaking, the more specific the information on the wine's origin, the higher quality the wine is supposed to be.

Why all this fuss over where a wine was made and where the grapes were grown? Simply because most of the differing characteristics in wine are due to the soil and climate in which the grapes were grown. For example, almost all wine-producing countries, and for that matter almost all wine-producing areas of California, plant and grow the Barberra grape. But wines made from this grape vary widely in taste and quality according to where the grape was grown and under what conditions.

Another example is the Gamay grape, known in California for its use in Gamay Beaujolais wine, and the grape most common in the French region of Beaujolais. You will find great differences between California's Gamay Beaujolais and French Beaujolais wine. California's is heavier and more robust, has taken much longer to pick up its earthiness, and will keep longer once it is opened than French Beaujolais, all because of the different soils and climates in which the grape is grown.

We would imagine, though, that much of the wine you purchase, especially that bought for everyday consumption, will not be so specifically labeled as to where the grapes were grown. More likely it will be labeled by

Wine regions of France

a state, probably California, because, of the forty-four states in this country producing wine, 80 percent of it comes from California. You will find that most of the wines we recommend you begin with are relatively inexpensive and are labeled as coming from California or an area within California. And absolutely the only way you can make a judgment about these wines is by trying them—not by reading the label.

Similarly, French wines that are labeled with a broad geographical name—Burgundy or Bordeaux, for example—must be tasted before a judgment can be made. Such a generic name really tells you only what type of wine is in the bottle, and almost nothing about its character.

To be sure, you know that a red Burgundy, for example, is going to be fairly heavy and dry with a fragrant bouquet, but that is about all. Hence, you must try the wine and remember the label, rather than trying to find a wine you like by reading the label.

While we are discussing French labels we might as well tell you that we are not very impressed with either the French or the Italian wine control laws. Certainly if a French wine is labeled Chablis you can be sure it has come from that district. But we are skeptical of the notation "appellation contrôlée" (which means the wine has been produced under certain regulations) and some others, because they seem to us to be carelessly awarded these days. We do not take them to mean very much.

Along these lines it might interest you
48   that *The Los Angeles Times* reported on

June 20, 1974, a major French wine labeling scandal. Millions of bottles of low-grade wine from the southeast of France were altered in color and their documents falsified in order to pawn the wine off as "Bordeaux Supérieur"— wine that has passed a number of quality tests. The French claimed that they impounded all of the misrepresented wine before it could be exported, and so they may have, but we wonder still how much mislabeled wine was shipped before the crime was discovered. What we are telling you is that we take all of these foreign awards and designations with a few grains of salt, and we recommend that you do the same.

Probably the biggest help in reading French wine labels is a little knowledge of French geography. There are the larger regions, Burgundy, Bordeaux, Chablis, Champagne, Cognac; and there are the smaller regions within the larger ones, which we could call areas: Beaujolais in Burgundy, Médoc in Bordeaux, Chateauneuf-du-Pape in the Côtes-du-Rhône area, which itself is in Burgundy, and so on. Knowing the names of these areas and their general location is important so you will have some idea of what you are buying, but the greatest advantage to knowing a smattering of French geography is to help you distinguish one wine from the other. If you have a "peg" or a "pigeon-hole" to help you remember something, it is a lot easier.

With German wines, as with French, geographical knowledge is also invaluable, mainly because German wines are similarly named for an area and not a grape. It is a good method because the same variety of grape planted in different areas produce quite distinguishable wines—that is, wines with different characteristics. For example, the Johannisberg Riesling grape, the most widely planted grape in Germany, produces widely varying wine according to where it is grown.

Recently Germany has passed some new laws on wine labeling, and Germans are now probably as strict in their labeling, or more so, than any other country. *Tafelwein* (table wine) is the lowest type, and is usually not exported, being reserved for home consumption. *Qualitaetswein* is next in line in quality, and bottles must be numbered as official proof that the contents meet certain specifications. The very best German wines are labeled *qualitaetswein mit praedikat*; these include their estate-bottled wines.

A further quality control is signified by terms that refer to the time of grape harvest that produced the wine. *Spätlese* is the most common of these terms; it means "late picking." You could have, for example, a Piesporter Spätlese, which would be from a late picking of the crop from which the wine was made, and would therefore supposedly be superior to a plain Piesporter. The term *Auslese* means a wine has been made from specially selected bunches of grapes. The next higher term, *Beerenauslese*, means wine made from hand-selected berries from specially selected bunches of grapes. *Trockenbeerenauslese* is a term assigned to wine produced when the grape harvest was done so late in the season that the grapes were almost raisins.

50 Generally, the higher the designation and the

later and more selective the picking, the rarer and more expensive the wine.

Thus, as far as the labeling information about where a wine was made is concerned, the more specific it is, the better you will be able to judge what you are getting. But as always, it is the taste test that must serve as the ultimate judging factor.

The other information that will appear on a wine label is the name of the concern that made or produced the wine. Our experience has been that many neophyte wine drinkers are hesitant to change brands, once they find a single wine that they like. That is, when they discover a wine that suits their palate from a certain winery, they buy all their wines from that brand. In the business field this is called "product identification." It is not something we recommend.

We find that the name of the winery, the brand name, is useful more as a means of identification than as a recommendation, a designation rather than an endorsement. In other words, for us a brand name merely distinguishes one wine from another.

For example, we think that Gallo Hearty Burgundy is an excellent buy when both price and quality are taken into consideration. But Gallo also produces some wines we do not think are so great, and which we are not in the habit of buying.

Having said this, we have to go on to say that there are certain wineries that maintain a high standard of excellence throughout their complete wine list. Inglenook Winery is the first example that comes to mind. We do not

say we recommend every wine that Inglenook
produces, just that the wine of theirs we like
the least is still not too bad.

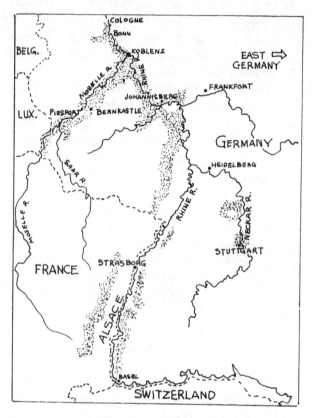

Wine regions of Germany

You will notice when you read the chapter,
"Our Favorite Wines," where we list some of
our favorite wines, that we suggest you buy your
first wines from France and Germany and other
foreign countries through the importer's brand
name. In that particular case the brand name is a
useful tool for beginners, because it guaran-
52 tees a certain standard of quality. Once you

become more adept at buying wine, however, its value diminishes, except as a means of identification. As we have said before, and will say again and again, the one basic way to increase your knowledge about wine is to buy some and try it!

That brings us, finally, to an interesting point concerning wine quality. As in many other industries today, conglomerates have taken over much of the wine industry, buying control of both well-known and lesser-known wineries. Conglomerates, by their very nature, are interested only in making money, which is to say selling more and more wine. They know they will not be able to sell an inferior product over the long haul, but we firmly believe they are commited to quality only to the degree that it will pay off in dollars and cents.

The smaller wineries, on the other hand, those that are controlled by one person, one family, or a small group of friends, have had—and probably always will have—a commitment to quality for its own sake; here personal reputations are at stake, and a good reputation is the dearest thing a person can own. In our opinion, the smaller wineries are the hope of the future for those of us who are interested in wine of high quality, because these are run by people who take pride in their work, regardless of corporate profits, tax shelters, and proxy votes.

One of the most controversial aspects of wine, and one that is the cause of much wine snobbery, is vintage. Vintage means "year of harvest"; it is as simple as that. You will not find the vintage date listed on many wine

53

labels because it is not a requirement, and in fact a vintage date cannot be listed unless all the grapes used to produce the wine were harvested in the same year. Thus, a 1968 vintage means that all the grapes were harvested in 1968.

Vintage has importance in both foreign and domestic wines, but with a different emphasis for each. The prime importance of vintage for foreign wines, and the point where wine drinkers mention the phrase, "a good year," has to do with the widely variable climatic conditions in most wine-growing areas, notably in France. Indeed, weather conditions change so drastically from year to year that there can be particularly good years and particularly bad ones, and these extremes are what make vintage especially important. Normally, despite what the wine snobs say, vintage is not that critical; important, but not critical.

Logically enough, when there is a particularly good or bad year in a region, it is true for all vineyards in that region, not just one. But a good reason for not being a slave to vintage is the fact that bad wines are made in good years, and good wines are made in bad years.

Because climatic conditions in California are much more uniform than those in most other wine-growing regions of the world (in fact, California grape growers speak of "micro-climate," the climate of one particular field), knowing the good and bad years is not of too much help when selecting a wine.

However, a vintage date on a bottle of California wine does tell you how long the wine has been aged. And because aging has quite a bit to do with the character of a wine, in this case it is quite helpful to know the vintage. If you are looking for a wine for tonight's dinner, and you know, for example, that a vintage Cabernet Sauvignon needs to be aged a minimum of five years, you will not buy a vintage that is only three years old.

Obviously, the reason for the importance of vintage with respect to foreign wines also applies to California, but to a much lesser degree. And the reason for its importance for California wines also holds true, but to a lesser degree, for foreign wines.

On the other hand, the absence of a vintage date on a bottle of wine, especially a California wine, does not mean that the wine is inferior. This is true because of the expertise in blending wines that California winemakers have developed. The taste of one particular wine is apt to be the same season after season. One year 40 percent of a certain grape might be used to achieve the desired taste, while the next year only 20 percent of that grape might be used to get the same taste. Thus, you can be fairly safe in assuming that one winery's Burgundy, for example, will taste the same from year to year. The Christian Brothers Winery is recognized throughout the industry as one of the best in this regard.

Lack of a vintage date is also no indication that the wine is too young to be good, for through blending the winemaker is able to make certain wines age more rapidly than normal. For example, Zinfandels age much faster than most other red wines, which is the reason they are used quite frequently in the **55** blending process. Pinot Noir needs to be aged much longer, but how much longer depends upon how much of the Pinot Noir grape is used in the wine. If there is a relatively small amount of the Pinot Noir grape used, say 60 percent, that wine may be fully aged in three years. If there is a large amount of the Pinot Noir grape used, say 80 percent, the wine may have to be held as long as five years or more. So do not be afraid to try the nonvintaged wines; in fact, do try them, for you will discover some very fine wines at very reasonable prices.

It must also be said that every once in a while there *is* a particularly good year, just as the wine snobs declare. Some of the generally accepted good years for French wine are 1959, 1961, 1968, and 1973. In Germany, 1971 was a superb wine year. If you happen upon a wine from a certain year that you like, the chances are that wine of that same vintage from other wineries in the same area will be equally as good. The wines may not taste the same, but they will be equally as good because the acid and tannin contents will be similar. Likewise, even though it may have been a good year, remember we have warned you that some winemakers can still produce an inferior wine. And even in bad years, as 1963 and 1964 were supposed to have been, some winemakers will come up with excellent wines.

There is another reason why some wineries omit any dating on their wine labels, but a not-so-commendable one. From people within the wine industry, we have learned that many wineries are not aging their wines nearly

as long as they used to, primarily because the

demand for wine these days has become greater than the production can supply. Because the demand is so great, wineries are releasing for sale wines that are quite young—too young, in our opinion. This is just one more reason why you should rely upon your own tastes, and should not expect the information on a wine label to guarantee you a wine you like.

Riesling   Burgundy   Bordeaux

Wine bottle *can* indicate origin

There is a profusion of other printing on a wine label, most of it totally irrelevant. For example, the word "premium" is widely used, and it is supposed to mean that the wine so labeled is a cut above the average. In fact it is usually nothing more than an attempt to charge you more per bottle than the wine is worth. Are you impressed by the medals and ribbons so prominently displayed by many wineries? Do not be, for almost every winery has boxes full of them. Award winners? Often the most disappointing wines we taste. The French term *gran vin* is another case in point. It is like saying "fine wine," but of course our question is, according to whose taste? It means nothing and is no more than some advertising promoter's desire to impress you with superlatives. So beware of meaningless phrases and terms on the wine label, for they can easily lead you astray.

To draw all this together then, the important information on a wine label is: where, by whom, and when. Where were the grapes grown? Who made the wine? When did they make it? Sort out this information, weigh it against your past experiences, use it as a guideline. But let *your* palate be the final judge. Taste is what it all comes down to in the end.

Caring for Your Wine

About a year ago a housewife came into the store visibly upset and handed us a bottle of Barton and Guestier Chateauneuf-du-Pape. "What's wrong with this?" she wailed. "We have two cases of it, and already I've had to throw out three bottles. I'm afraid it's all bad."

We looked at the label, checked the vintage, and immediately had a pretty good notion of what the problem was. At our customer's request we opened the wine and tasted it, because it was possible that the wine had spoiled, but our original suspicions were confirmed. The wine had all the proper characteristics—beautiful balance, good color, outstanding aroma and bouquet—except the one it needed most, age. The wine was simply too young to be consumed, and that was the only thing wrong with it. Our customer needed to store the wine properly for about five years so it would reach its full maturity. By then she will have a great wine.

The immediate question is, then, how do you store wine? We suppose everyone has heard of those legendary wine cellars full of cobwebs and dust, where hundreds of bottles

59

of aged wine lays in racks, and where seven workers died while tunneling the thing out of the limestone rocks. If you own one of these wine cellars you are quite fortunate. If you do not, you are not much worse off.

Old wine cellar romanticized in literature

The most important factor in storing wine so that it will age, rather than spoil, is to keep the temperature constant to within a few degrees. Wild fluctuations in temperature will destroy wine, so you must control that temperature. You could, if you so desired, invest a lot of money in humidifiers and air conditioners, but you do not have to.

The simplest and cheapest way to store wine is to build a rack or bin out of small sewer tiles, the kind made out of red clay. For some reason, which you physicists could tell us if we cared to know, the temperature inside one of the bottle-sized sewer tiles varies only slightly, even though the surrounding air temperature may vary as much as 20 to 30 degrees. So if you construct a rack of sewer tiles so they and the bottles inside them lie flat, you will have an extremely effective storage system. You can store your wine there and forget it until you want to drink it, knowing it will be aging safely and in no danger of spoiling.

Storage rack easily constructed from clay tiles
and a few boards

If you have something against sewer tiles, you can purchase wine racks in a variety of styles from most hardware and department stores. There are dozens of them on the market, made from a wide assortment of materials. Unfortunately, these usually lack the insulating properties of the sewer tiles, but if you place them in a good spot they will serve adequately.

Whatever your rack looks like, put it in a **61**

dark corner where the temperature is fairly constant and reasonably cool. If you have a closet built into an inside wall, that is a good place. A corner of your garage or basement will also work well as long as it is not subjected to a tremendous heat build-up in the summer. What you should *not* do is place your wine rack on top of your refrigerator, because almost all refrigerators have a strong flow of warm air over the top and that is highly undesirable.

You further should choose a spot for your rack that is reasonably dark most of the time. You do not want very much light to reach your wine, not even artificial light. Darkness also provides the advantage of keeping your wine out of your brother-in-law's sight—unless he is something of a snoop.

Perhaps you are wondering why we recommend that you construct a wine cellar or storage system at all. Why can't you simply drink your wine and forget it?

There are two very basic reasons. The first is that, as a general rule, red wines improve with age. Often the only difference between a fine vintage wine and an inexpensive jug wine is the length of time each has been aged. So the first reason for storing your wines is to improve them, and to do this you must take some precautions to insure that the wine will mature, rather than spoil.

The second reason for having a wine storage system is an economic one. Let us assume that you like to have available an especially good red wine for especially important occasions. If the wine you want is available (which it probably will not be), you are going to be charged a good many dollars for having the winery, or the wine merchant, store and age the wine for you. Therefore, the simplest way to lower the cost of finer red wines is to buy them when they are young and still fairly inexpensive, store them yourself in your new wine cellar, and have them on hand a few years later when that certain special occasion arises.

As an example, we recently served with dinner a Zinfandel that we bought for 95¢ about six years ago and had stored all this time. We decanted it into a nice container, and after everyone had sampled it we casually asked for their opinions on the wine. Most of our guests thought it was a Cabernet Sauvignon, and one woman—who knows good wines—was sure it was an expensive Bordeaux. Perhaps it was not quite fair to fool our guests like that, but it did prove a point; that proper aging of almost any red wine is what makes the difference.

Incidentally, if you want a better wine right now, before your wine cellar has existed long enough to be effective, we recommend that you buy a vintage that guarantees that the wine has been aged a while. For example, for the same amount of money you might have a choice between a young Cabernet Sauvignon and a four-year-old Zinfandel. We suggest you buy the Zinfandel if you want to drink the wine immediately, because its age will make it better for present consumption than the younger Cabernet Sauvignon.

You may have noticed that we have been discussing red wines until now. That is because white wines should be treated differently.

One of our customers who has a fantastic wine cellar called us in recently to check her wines, because some of them had spoiled. After examining her collection we had to discard twenty-eight bottles, all of them white wines. We could tell they were spoiled by the color (darkish brown), but we opened a few just to be sure. And they certainly were spoiled.

The problem is that most white wines do not age well beyond the time the winery has held them. Indeed, it takes very special care to improve them in the bottle. Usually, the younger they are, the better, and you must have very special facilities and perfect conditions even to keep them at their peak. So we suggest that you buy only the amount of white wine you can use within six months or so. Obviously, some will hold longer than that, but six months seems to us a safe time limit.

There are other techniques to learn about buying and storing wine. If you can find the cold hard cash to buy your wine by the case, you will discover that most states allow for a discount ranging from 5 to 15 percent. In California, for example, the case discount is 10 percent. This applies to mixed cases as well as to cases of all one wine, just as long as you purchase a full case, whether it be twelve bottles of fifths, six half-gallons, or four gallons.

By the way, do not think there is anything wrong with aging wine that you have purchased in half-gallons or gallons. As a matter of fact, jug wines will almost always **64** age faster than anything else because they are blended by the winery to do so. Two or three years of additional aging on most bulk wines will improve them to the degree that they will be comparable to many wines five times as expensive. Just keep in mind that once you open a red wine you should drink it all within about a week's time. So if you open a gallon jug and do not think you can use it within that time limit, you will have to rebottle it into smaller bottles. If you try the rebottling, make certain you fill the bottle all the way into the neck, so that some of the wine is forced out as you insert the cork. That way there will be no air left in the bottle to cause oxidation and spoilage.

While mentioning jug wines we want to let you in on a little trick that will make quite a difference in their taste. When you open a gallon of red wine, do it the day before you want to drink it. Pour out a glassful, then recap the jug and let it sit on the kitchen counter overnight. This allows the wine to "breathe," dissipating the acids. The older a wine is, the less breathing it needs, but even a twenty-year-old wine needs a little time to air, say an hour or so. Therefore, it is a good idea to open all red wines long enough before you serve them that they will have the chance to breathe.

It is certainly possible, though not likely, that occasionally you might have a bottle of wine spoil. If you think this has happened to you, do not be afraid to taste the wine in question to see for sure. It will not be poison, even if it is spoiled. The worst it could be is vinegar and it will not hurt you. If it is vinegar, or is on the way to becoming vinegar, you do not have to throw it out. You can use it as wine vinegar on salads, for that is exactly what it is—wine vinegar.

One of the indications that wine has spoiled is a moldy cork, but only if the mold has gathered on the bottom of the cork, and even then it is not a sure sign. You will still have to taste the wine to find out. Just make sure you clean the inside of the bottle neck with a towel or a napkin before you pour any of the wine, so that none of the moldy taste gets into the wine. If there is mold on top of the cork, there is not much reason to worry. It simply means that somewhere along the road that the bottle of wine has traveled moisture has been present. Again, just be sure to clean the bottle well before pouring.

Keeping open bottles of wine in the refrigerator will retard spoilage, so we suggest you do just that. If it is a red wine, it is then advisable to remove the bottle from the refrigerator about an hour before serving in order to bring the wine's temperature up to 60 or 65°. That will give you the benefit of a fuller bouquet and aroma, and a smoother taste. White wines should be served colder, so it is fine to leave them under refrigeration until serving time.

The temperature at which you serve wine is very important. We suspect that almost everyone has heard the old advice that red wine should be served at room temperature. If you take that to mean the temperature of the average American house, you are dead wrong. The temperature referred to is *wine* room temperature, which should be about 62°. In

our opinion there is nothing worse than

serving a red wine at a temperature of 75° with a hot meal in a hot room. Well, maybe there is something worse—serving a red wine at 42° under the same conditions. Therefore, if the wine has been refrigerated, let it stand in the room for an hour or so. And if the wine feels warm to you when you take it out of your wine cellar or storage area, an hour of refrigeration will chill it to the proper degree.

On occasion you might find a few crystals inside the neck of the wine bottle. They could be from something simple like a stabilizer that the winery has used, something like cream of tartar. All you can do is open the wine and sample it. If it tastes good to you the chances are that the crystals are from a stabilizer. On the other hand, under extreme heat and rough handling, wine will form actual crystals that indicate spoilage. So if the wine tastes "vinegary" when you sample it, you are the not-so-proud possessor of mis-treated wine. It does happen; we recently had to return three cases of wine to one of our distributors because of crystalization.

Some time ago we watched an episode on the television show "Columbo" in which the owner of a winery had a wine-tasting party for four of his close friends, all so-called wine connoisseurs. The elaborate ritual these men went through to open and decant their supposedly rare wines was—to us—the height of affectation. It was pure wine snobbery and it had nothing to do with the correct handling of a bottle of wine (although it did provide a good mystery plot for Columbo).

The care with which you handle your

wine is critical, but no elaborate rituals or affectations are needed—simply care. And the care you use to handle old rare wine serves one purpose and one purpose only—to keep sediment out of the liquid.

We think it stands to reason that you should not toss any wine bottle around like a baseball. Just treat it gently and you will have done your job. If the wine is old, and has been stored on its side at an angle, as it should have been, try to maintain the angle as you open the bottle and pour it out. Take your time, pour slowly, and stop pouring at the first sign of sediment.

The oldest bottle of wine we have ever experienced was about seventy years old. It was quite delicious in spite of what we consider too much age, but it contained a lot of sediment. We removed the cork a day ahead of time and stored the wine on a tilt of about forty-five degrees to allow the sediment to settle into one corner of the bottle. Then, when we decanted the wine, we maintained the forty-five-degree angle as best we could and the sediment remained in place. Just before the sediment started to come out we stopped pouring. The remainder of the wine we filtered through cheesecloth into a separate glass (it amounted to no more than that), and kept it for ourselves.

You should bear in mind, of course, that wine sediment will not hurt you—it is simply distasteful. Sediment is merely an accumulation of the tannins and acids that cause the wine to age. With a modicum of care you can keep it out of your wine.

There are probably as many types of

wine-bottle openers as there are wines, and there is only a little to say about any of them. The best we have ever seen is the opener that has two springy prongs that slide alongside the cork, between the cork and the bottle neck, allowing you to gently rock the cork out of the bottle. The advantages are two: you can rock the cork and not the wine, and you do not get any flecks of cork in the wine.

Other than that opener, what you use is a corkscrew. The features of a good corkscrew are fairly simply: (1) a sharp point (because a dull point will push tiny pieces of cork into the wine); (2) a broad spiral screw (a thinner spiral pulls out of the cork too easily); and (3) some method of leverage to help you slip the cork out of the bottle without making like King Kong. Incidentally, if the corkscrew pulls out of the cork while the cork is still inside the bottle, as sometimes happens, especially with older corks, *with care* you can re-insert the corkscrew across the original threads you have cut. With any luck at all the cork should then be gripped firmly enough for removal.

One important "no-no" concerning bottle openers: never use the type of opener that pumps air into the bottle under pressure. It is something like stomping on the kitchen floor while there is a cake baking in the oven. Pumping air pressure into the wine bottle is also like detonating a bomb inside of it. You will ruin the wine more often than not, and you run the additional risk of exploding the bottle.

In all honesty we must admit that there might come a time when even we would be tempted to go through some elaborate ritual to open a bottle of wine. We have in front of us a news clipping about a wine auction in Geneva, Switzerland, where someone paid $399 for six bottles of Chambertin 1929 and $782 for twelve bottles of Chateau Latour 1945. Had we been foolish enough to pay that much for a few bottles of wine, we would most likely be foolish enough to indulge in some pomp and circumstance when we opened it.

Ordering Wine
in a Restaurant

Two of our regular customers came into the store one day, young women who work a few days a week as showgirls in Las Vegas and live the remainder of the time in our area. They were having some rather special guests for dinner that evening, so they spent some time searching through our more expensive wines. Eventually they picked out a 1972 Pommard from France that sold for almost $12 a bottle.

When they brought the bottle to us and asked what we thought of their choice, we explained that their selection would have been excellent if their dinner were being served six years from now, but that at this moment they would be much better off with a $5 bottle of California wine.

One of the women could not believe it. She said that she picked that particular wine because it had been served to her in one of the very high-priced Las Vegas restaurants, ordered by her escort, who seemed to know what he was doing. Then the other woman threw in her two cents' worth. She claimed that the wine had not tasted good to her when she had had it in Vegas, but she thought her

71

palate must have been off, because it had set the men back $40 a bottle.

We finally persuaded the women to buy another wine, one we felt would go well with the dinner they were preparing, and we were pleased to learn a few days later that they had found our recommendation much better than that of their Las Vegas escorts.

Our point of course, is that you should be extremely wary when ordering wine in restaurants because you can very easily be taken. We would hope that restauranteurs would feel some obligation to their customers to provide them with good, honest, drinkable wines, but we have, unfortunately, found many instances where the wine list included wines that could not possibly be any good.

We had an incident ourselves that revolved around a two-year-old Pommard. We saw it on the wine list of a very good restaurant at $28 per bottle. When questioned about it, the wine steward hesitantly admitted that he knew the wine was not drinkable, and would not be for another eight or ten years, but he offered the excuse that it was what his customers wanted. We claimed he had an obligation to serve his customers not only the finest food, but the finest wines also, but we are afraid we did not convince him.

Let us simply say that any time you pay $40 for a bottle of wine, you have been "ripped off."

Wine stewards, or *sommeliers*, if we may use the French word with the magical ring to it, are well aware that most of their customers know next to nothing about wine. With a simple curl of the lip they can intimidate most of us into buying an expensive wine. So if you do not know that certain wines will not be fully aged until a certain time period has elapsed, it is very possible for you to be cheated.

It is not all the fault of the wine steward. He is under some pressure to sell the expensive stuff, just as a clothing salesman tries to get you to buy the $16 shirt rather than the $8 one. As in all cases when you are spending your money, it is a matter of "buyer beware."

Therefore, if you want to be *assured* of getting a wine that will please you, stick with something you know. If there is nothing on the wine list you recognize, tell the waiter what you like and perhaps he will be able to come close to it.

We suppose that you have all experienced the ritual that waiters and wine stewards go through when they bring a bottle of wine to your table. The bottle is usually wrapped in a cloth, which is ceremoniously whipped off as the label is revealed. After the cork is drawn it is presented to you to smell, then a sip is poured for the host to sample, and at his nod the res of the glasses on the table are filled.

One evening in 1974, in the finest restaurant in our area, a man sitting at a table near ours deliberately made a shambles of the entire routine. When the waiter presented the cork, the gentleman sniffed it, as he was supposed to do, but then he put the cork in his mouth, chomped off a piece, and began chewing, meanwhile moaning appropriate noises of delight. After a few seconds of this

73

he grabbed the bottle out of the flabbergasted waiter's hand and chug-a-lugged a full third of it.

Besides reducing a snobbish waiter practically to tears, our hero accomplished something else—he put the whole business of wine snobbery into the proper perspective. Believe us when we say we have nothing personal against wine stewards. We simply say that too many of them put on airs over something as down-to-earth as a bottle of wine.

There are occasions when the waiter or wine steward can be very helpful, as when you tell him what you like in a wine. You are then asking his expert advice, and it becomes a matter of professional pride, not a matter of one-upping the snobbish customer. We have also found that if you profess complete ignorance about his wine list, inform him graciously that you do not want to lose a small fortune on a bottle of wine, and throw yourself on his mercy, you have a better than fair chance of coming out all right.

A good wine steward should know, as you do by now, that a red wine needs to be opened and allowed to breathe for an hour or so. Therefore, he would not recommend, nor would you order, a bottle of red wine unless you are prepared to wait, simply because the wine otherwise would not have time to breathe before being served and would not be even close to its full flavor and bouquet.

Incidentally, if you have reservations at a restaurant and intend to honor them, it is perfectly permissible to order your wine in advance, assuming you know what you will want. It can then be opened a few hours before you arrive for the necessary breathing time. In fact, we think a restaurant would be delighted to have you order in advance, since it tells them they will have a patron that evening who will enjoy their service to the utmost.

If you want to put on airs to impress someone, you might be tempted to send back the bottle of wine that the waiter brings you. Believe us when we say that the only person you could possibly impress is your guest, and that in itself is highly unlikely. You will not fool yourself, of course, and you will look like an idiot to the waiter.

The chances are almost nil that you would ever in your lifetime have to send back a bottle of wine because it is bad. Fine restaurants have superior wine storage facilities in this day and age, and we believe that most of them take good care of their stock. Even most mediocre restaurants take care of their wine.

If ever a wine does taste bad to you, examine yourself first. Are you showing off for someone else's benefit? Have you had too much hard liquor, thus throwing your palate off? Have you been smoking heavily, another destroyer of taste? Did you, in fact, know what you were ordering, or did you take a shot in the dark?

If you answer all these questions appropriately and still think the wine is bad, then you ask the wine steward to taste the wine himself and be reasonably assured that he will give you a truthful answer. In that instance you are again calling upon his professionalism, rather than trying to one-up him, and he will almost always give you a straight answer.

Incidentally, we want to stress the fact that just two or three cocktails before dinner are enough to throw your wine palate off quite a bit. One of the things that makes wine drinking so pleasurable is the discreet nuances of taste that can be developed. Compared to such fine distinctions between wines, drinking hard liquor is like taking a slug of gasoline; so if you want to experience the more subtle pleasures of a fine wine, stay away from liquor for a few hours before dinner.

Thus you have the guidelines for ordering wine in a restaurant. Stick with what you know, or tell the waiter what you like and let him try to come close to it. Do not be intimidated into buying something expensive. And treat your palate gently for a few hours beforehand. By following these simple suggestions, ordering wine becomes a pleasure rather than a chore; and, after all, pleasure is what wine is all about.

Wine-Tasting Parties

If you want to have a lot of fun, and in the process learn something about wine, host a wine-tasting party. It is a great way to enjoy the company of your friends, and it does not have to become a gigantic Hollywood production. You can have a delightful—and delicious—time doing it in a warm, low-key manner.

A tasting party is for people who enjoy good wine, good food, and good conversation. With that in mind, when you make up your guest list you should use the same common sense you would when you decide who you are going to invite to any party you are having. In this case, we advise you to invite only those friends you think will enjoy the wine tasting. This is not the kind of gathering with which you repay all your social obligations. If you have friends who have no interest in wine, or who get no enjoyment out of it, settle your social debt with them at some other time. Reserve this party for wine lovers.

The rules we give you for holding a party of this sort are designed to help everyone enjoy themselves, so it is not necessary to follow them rigidly if they do not suit you. 77

Remember, the party is for fun. But we do think our guidelines will make it easier on you, while allowing everyone to have a good time.

If by now you are seriously considering hosting a party of this nature, you are probably already counting your wine glasses to see if you have enough. Our advice is to stop worrying about it. There is an old saying that any glass is suitable for wine, as long as it does not have a hole in it.

The best all-purpose wine glass shape

Some glasses, of course, are more suitable than others. An excellent all-around choice for wine is a clear eight-ounce, tulip-shaped, stemmed glass. First of all, this glass will show off your wine to the best advantage, and, let's face it, a person eats and drinks with his eyes as well as his mouth. We also eat, so to speak, with our nose, which is to say that smell plays a very important part in our enjoyment of what we put into our mouth.

The tulip-shaped glass collects the aroma and bouquet of the wine better than other glasses. Therefore, when you put the glass to your mouth to take a drink, your nose picks up the collected aroma and bouquet and adds to your enjoyment. The stem is desirable because it keeps the heat of your hand from warming the wine.

If you do not have any stemware, and cannot justify buying any before the party, the next best glass to use is a plain old water glass. What you should not use, in our opinion, is a champagne glass or a martini glass. Because these flare at the top they dissipate, rather than collect, the aroma and bouquet of the wine, and you thus lose one of the important ingredients of your tasting party.

Probably the most neglected part of home wine-tasting parties is maintaining control of the action. There are a few simple suggestions that will enable you to do that. First, either pour the wine yourself or hire a bartender to do it for you, and if you hire a bartender be sure you tell him exactly how you want the wine poured and when. Absolutely do not allow people to help themselves, because if you do it is an even-money bet that something will go wrong: someone will drink the wines in the wrong order, or will take more than his share and short-change another guest, or he may dump a bottle of Burgundy on your new white shag rug.

It also helps if you can avoid congestion in the room and give people some breathing room. A good way to do this is to put the wine on a table on one side of the room, and

79

have the cheese, bread, and water on a table on the other side. Your guests are thus forced to move, and everyone will have a more pleasant time. This is not critical, of course, but the idea is to maintain control of the situation and we think this is a good way to do it.

When you are pouring the wine, serve only about three-fourths of a glass of the whites, and only one-half of a glass of the reds. You pour less of the red wines because they are the ones with the aroma and bouquet that you want to collect inside the top of the glass, and also because the added room in the glass gives red wines the chance they need to breathe so that the tannins and acids will dissipate.

Fill glass ¾ full of white wine and ½ full of red wine

We further suggest that you open the bottles beforehand, have them cooling in the refrigerator (see the fourth chapter, "Caring for Your Wine," for serving temperatures), and already wiped off. Some experts tell you to leave the metal foil around the neck of the bottle for the sake of appearance. We think that is mere affectation, and also slightly dangerous, because if any of the wine touches the metal foil, it may impart a metallic taste to the wine. The foil certainly cannot help the wine, so we take it completely off the bottle.

If you are anything like us, one of the first questions you ask yourself when you are hosting any kind of party is, "How much is this going to cost? How much of everything do I buy?" We have a rule of thumb that seems to work fairly well for wine-tasting parties. For a three- or four-hour party you will need one-half bottle of wine for each person you are serving—*as a minimum.* Therefore, for eight people the least amount of wine you should buy is four bottles. Some people, quite naturally, will not drink their share, but others will drink more, and we think it is better to be safe than to be embarrassed. If you can have more wine, by all means have it. After all, what your guests do not drink, you can afterwards.

Incidentally, you may have heard somewhere that some of the wineries will supply you with free wine for your tasting party. As far as we know this is a false rumor. First of all it is against the law, and, second, wineries do not have enough wine to sell, let alone give away. What they will give you is free advice, although naturally they are interested in promoting their own products and therefore could not in any way be accused of impartiality.

As far as anything else that you need to make your party a success, there is very little.

We always have ice water and glasses on hand, along with some cubed French bread or some unsalted crackers. We suggest to our guests that after drinking each wine they clear their palates with a little bread and water. We also like to allow twenty to thirty minutes between the different wines, so that people have a chance for a second glass if they so desire.

We have tried all kinds of wine parties. We have had our selection made only from those wines available in half-gallons, in which case we used carafes or decanters. We have also had parties where every wine was from one area; all from the Napa Valley, for example, or all from France. We have also tried parties at which we had each of our wines from a different country. We first served a Soave from Italy, then a Rosé from Portugal, a Médoc from France, a Burgundy from Spain, and ended with a Madeira from the island of Madeira. All of these parties were fun, and as you gain some confidence in your wine palate we hope you will try your hand at a few of them.

As far as cheeses go, we think it is appropriate to serve a wine and a cheese from the same country sometimes—a Gorgonzola with Chianti wine, for example. We also like bleu cheese with red wines, but there are others that go just as well, as you will see from our sample parties.

You will notice in our suggested parties that we make specific suggestions about which cheese to serve with which wine. We do this for a reason. We serve a light cheese with a light wine so that neither overpowers the other. We strive for a balance between the two, where one complements the other. As an additional means of control for your party, if you think there is the slightest chance you will become confused about which cheese goes with which wine, by all means number both the wine bottles and the cheese plates. Get yourself some tags or some tape and place corresponding numbers on both the wines and the cheeses.

One last item that is extremely important: you simply must serve the lightest wine of the grouping first, and the heaviest wine last. If you do not, the heavier-bodied wine will overpower the lighter-bodied one, and you will completely lose any nuances of flavor, body, and smell that the lighter wine might have. We have listed our wines in the appropriate order, so be sure to follow it. In case you want to eliminate one of our selections, eliminate either the first or the last, but not any in the middle.

The first party we have outlined is for rank beginners; we tell you exactly what to buy. We do the same for the second party, but the choices are a bit more expensive. The third list of suggestions is different. By the time you are ready for your third party you will have your own likes and dislikes, and we have therefore given you a list from which you can select the wines you would like to sample.

Just remember that not only are you trying to learn something about wines, you are also trying to have fun.

Beginner's Party

* Italian Swiss Colony Grenache Rosé, with American cheese
* Italian Swiss Colony Chablis, or Gold Seal Chablis, with Jack cheese
* Almadén Zinfandel, with Swiss cheese
* Gallo Hearty Burgundy, with Gouda cheese
* Paul Masson Madeira, with Muenster cheese, white grapes, and sliced Red Delicious apples

Second-Level Party

* Charles Krug Grey Riesling, with Muenster cheese
* Wente Brothers Le Blanc de Blancs, with Brie cheese
* Almadén Gamay Beaujolais, with Camembert cheese
* Inglenook Zinfandel, with Tilsit cheese
* Louis Martini Cabernet Sauvignon, with a mixture of bleu cheese and cream cheese spread on a thin wheat cracker
* House of Koshu plum wine, with feta cheese and sliced Golden Delicious apples

Alternate Second-Level Party

Choose all the wines from one state or one region; for example, choose all Napa Valley wines, or all New York State wines.

* Chablis, with Jack cheese
* Beaujolais, with Port du Salut cheese

* Zinfandel, with mild cheddar cheese

* Petite Sirah, with an aged cheddar cheese
* Port, with sliced Golden Delicious apples

Third-Level Party

Select any combination of cheese and wine from each of the four categories. Just remember to serve them in the order listed.

* *Wines:*
    Armand Roux Sauterne
    Havemeyer Bernkasteler
    Bertani Soave
    Alianca Rosé
    Armand Roux Pouilly Fuissé
* *Cheese:*
    Swiss, Muenster, Gouda, or Jack
* *Wines:*
    Broglio Chianti Classico
    Ricasoli Valpolicella
    Martin LeVeque Beaujolais
    Armand Roux St.-Emilion
* *Cheese:*
    Provolone, Mozzarella, Camembert, or
    Brie
* *Wines:*
    Armand Roux Pommard
    Armand Roux Margaux
    Château de la Gardine Châteauneuf-du-
    Pape
    Barton and Guestier Nuits-St.-Georges
* *Cheese:*
    Gruyére, Liederkrantz, sharp cheddar,
    hickory-smoked cheddar, or Tilsit
* *Wines:*
    Paul Masson Crackling Rosé

85

Mumm Cordon Rouge Champagne
Martini and Rossi Asti Spumante
Rainwater Madeira

* *Cheese:*

> Mix cottage cheese, cream cheese, ricotta cheese with caviar, serve on thin wheat cracker

After you have tried a couple of our suggested wine and cheese lists, we hope you will strike out on your own, devising combinations that please your individual tastes. We do recommend that you limit your wine selection to no more than six for each party, simply because it becomes confusing and complicated when you have more. A good mixture is to serve two whites, one rosé, and three reds. But be careful not to have too wide a variety of types of wine.

Special care should be taken with your final selection—that is, the last wine served for the evening. We believe you should never serve both a sparkling wine and a dessert wine, but rather should have one or the other. Nor do we think you should serve two or three sparkling wines or dessert wines; limit your choice to only one of these.

These, then, are the guidelines. Along with some plain old common sense, they will help you to have a lot of fun while you discover some new wines and further enjoy a few of your old favorites.

Experiment, investigate, criticize, and praise, but most of all—enjoy!

Our Favorite Wines

Any list of somebody's favorite wines is highly subjective, to say the least. No two people have exactly the same tastes in wine. A look at the results of a wine-judging event will bear this out. The judges are all experts, so you would think they might have similar tastes. They do not. Rarely in these competitions do two or more judges rate the same wine as their number one choice. The "Grand Award Winner" almost invariably places first by being listed high—but not first—on everyone's list, rather than being the number one wine on the chart of three or four of the judges. The point is, of course, that not even the wine experts can agree.

Therefore, we offer this list of our favorites with humility, not expecting you to fall in love with all the wines we name, well aware that there are many excellent wines we have not named, and not presuming to tell you that our list is sacred. We are simply telling you that all things considered—price, quality, and availability—these are *our* favorites.

The wines on the list are not in a particular order of preference. We do like some better than others, of course, but we want

87

you to discover your favorites, not ours, so we have given them all equal rank.

All of our favorites are readily available throughout most of the country, but there will be certain places where your selection is limited, because not all states carry all brands. You may not be able to locate all the wines we have named, but if you can't find one brand of a certain variety, surely you can find another. That is why we have named three Pinot Chardonnays, for example, and three Zinfandels.

Along that same line, we feel that many people make the mistake of recommending wines that are exceptional, but that simply are not available anywhere. Sebastiani 1968 Pinot Noir is a perfect example. It is supposedly one of the best wines ever produced in California —but try to find it; it is absolutely unavailable. Because it would do you no good if we did recommend such wines, we have omitted them from our list.

We do not mention the price of any of the wines for a couple of reasons: first, wine prices vary according to the state in which you buy your wine; and second, prices do go up in this age of inflation. But price was one of the crucial criteria we considered in making up our list, and we think you will discover that we have truly stayed with the lower-priced wines.

We list California wines first, organizing them into five categories: white, red, rosé, sparkling, and appetizer/dessert wines. The brand name, or the winery name, is given first, followed by the name of the wine. The second listing is of imported wines from various countries, most of them from France.

Except for the wines from Germany and France, we have followed the same procedure for imported wines as we did for California wines; that is, we have given the brand first, followed by the type. For German and French wines we make a rather unusual suggestion, which has influenced the way we have constructed that portion of the list. Until you have some slight experience with German and French wines, we think you should buy only from the importers we have named; first, because the availability of these wines varies widely across the country, and second, because these brands give you a reasonable guarantee of quality. Should we name, for example, a red Bordeaux from some obscure chateau, the chances are that you will not be able to find it. By giving you two importers' brand names to choose from, we hope to give you a chance to get a good idea of the character of the wine, develop confidence in your own palate, and thus avoid intimidation. Once you know what to expect from a particular type of wine, you should by all means try the varieties available under lesser-known labels.

We further suggest that as you taste the various wines, either those on our list of those of your own choosing, you make notes of some sort so you will remember what you experienced (see the chapter, "Rating Your Wines"). And do not be surprised if a bottle of wine for which you paid $3 tastes every bit as good as, or better than, a bottle that sold for $6 or more.

NEW YORK & CALIFORNIA WINES

White Wines

* Mirassou: Gewürztraminer. A very spicy
wine with a slightly sweet finish.

* Charles Krug: Gewürztraminer. One of the
finest from Krug, but unavailable at
times. We believe Krug is one of the top
white wine producers in California.

* Almadén: Gewürztraminer. Very spicy and
very fruity; serve with a light dish, or with
cheese and fruit for dessert.

* Inglenook: Pinot Chardonnay. A heavy dry
wine that ranks at the top of our list.

* Almadén: Pinot Chardonnay (Estate
Bottled). Definitely worth what it costs.

* Mirassou: Pinot Chardonnay. This version
is particularly dry and tends to be heavy
for a white wine.

* Robert Mondavi: Riesling. Very lively with
a sweet finish; good with light meals and
light meats.

* Sebastiani: Sylvaner Riesling. A similar
slightly sweet finish, but fruitier; quite
refreshing.

* Charles Krug: Sylvaner Riesling. Still fruity,
but lighter; serve with chicken or fish.

* Almadén: Grey Riesling. Slightly sweet,
with a pleasing medium body.

* Charles Krug: Grey Riesling. Slightly sweet
also; medium-bodied, and always available.

* Inglenook: Sylvaner Riesling. This one has
a light and sweet finish.

* Charles Krug: Johannisberg Riesling. Heavier-bodied than the Grey Riesling.

* Paul Masson: Johannisberg Riesling. Slightly sweeter to go with light food.

* Paul Masson: Rhinecastle. A Riesling type, but a bit more sweet; priced for everyday use.

* Souverain: Green Hungarian. A varietal that is light and sweet.

* Weibel: Green Hungarian. Fruitier than the same variety by Souverain.

* Wente Brothers: le Blanc de Blancs. Very different; lively, fruity, slightly sweet; for those who like Rieslings, this one never misses.

* Christian Brothers: Château Lasalle. We find this a bit too sweet for dinner, but fine for dessert.

* Paul Masson: Emerald Dry. Despite the name, this wine is far from dry, but it is good.

* Wente Brothers: Dry Semillon. Compares favorably to a Barsac from France.

* Italian Swiss Colony: Chablis. One of the nicest at any price.

* Almadén: Chablis. Rates better than the price indicates, and therefore a good buy for daily use.

* Gallo: Chablis Blanc. A very good wine for the money, and also good for everyday drinking.

* Inglenook: Chenin Blanc. Always good quality, and quite dry and light.

* Weibel: Chenin Blanc. Excellent body and, **91**

again, quite dry, almost as dry as Pinot
Chardonnay.

* Wente Brothers: Sauvignon Blanc. A beau-
tiful dry white. In white wines, Wente
Brothers hold their own with Charles
King.

* Charles Krug: Moscato Di Canelli. Very
hard to find, but worth looking for.

Red Wines

* Beaulieu Vineyard: Cabernet Sauvignon. A
classic version of this popular varietal.

* Robert Mondavi: Cabernet Sauvignon.
Occasionally not available, but worth
looking for.

* Inglenook: Cabernet Sauvignon (Cask
Bottled). This is the pick of the crop and
has spent longer aging in wood than the
regular bottling. Hard to locate.

* Louis Martini: Cabernet Sauvignon. Fantastic body, which becomes like velvet after
four or five years of aging. For red
dinner wines, this is a consistently good
winery.

* Inglenook: Zinfandel. An excellent version
of this varietal; compare it to the less
expensive ones.

* Cribari: Zinfandel. Very good for the price.
Open the bottle a day ahead to improve
it.

* Italian Swiss Colony: Zinfandel. We buy
this by the case for everyday usage.
Italian Swiss Colony has excellent quality
throughout its line.

* Inglenook: Pinot Noir. Very hearty and full

of bite. You know you have tasted a Burgundy with this one.

* Almadén: Pinot Noir (Estate Bottled). This is worth the money in every way.

* Louis Martini: Barberra. A varietal with the real Burgundy bite to it.

* Christian Brothers: Pinot St.-George (Estate Bottled). One of the better table wines from the Napa Valley; this is a Burgundy-type varietal.

* Inglenook: Charbono (Estate Bottled). Another varietal of the Burgundy family, this is hearty and full of bite. Charbono has a long, long life.

* Wente Brothers: Petite Sirah. We believe this is Wente's best red wine.

* Concannon: Petite Sirah. An excellent version of this varietal in the Burgundy family.

* Gallo: Hearty Burgundy. Still the best generic Burgundy for the money.

* Louis Martini: Claret. An excellent dry wine for daily table use.

* Bully Hill: Claret. From New York State, this is more astringent than either California or French Clarets, but it is excellent if aged a bit in the bottle.

* Taylor: Lake Country Red. An impressive table wine from New York State.

* Louis Martini: Chianti. Dry, and as close to the Old World Chiantis as any of the California versions.

Rosé Wines

* Italian Swiss Colony: Grenache Rosé. The

true rosé of California; it will hold its own with much costlier versions.

* Almadén: Grenache Rosé. Compare this to Italian Swiss Colony's version and make your choice.

* Paul Masson: Crackling Rosé. Very delightful with its slight effervescence, and inexpensive; one of the best of this type.

Sparkling Wines

* Korbel: Champagne. The "extra dry" and "brut" both compare favorably with the finest of French Champagnes. This is the best made in California.

* Inglenook: Champagne. This has the earthy French character to it that we prefer.

* Taylor: Champagne. From New York state, this is excellent for the price.

* Jacques Bonet: Champagne. Made by Italian Swiss Colony, it is the best of the very inexpensive California Champagnes.

* Weibel: Moscato Spumante. Originally this was the Italian answer to French Champagne, though it is not intended to taste like Champagne; you will find it sweeter. An unusual treat.

Appetizer and Dessert Wines

* Christian Brothers: Muscatel. Muscatel has an infamous reputation as the "wino's" drink; but it is great as an appetizer.

* Almadén: Cocktail Sherry. This is a good basic Sherry at a reasonable price.

* Llords and Elwood: Dry Wit Sherry. Absolutely fantastic, and a must to try.
* Christian Brothers: Meloso. We think this is probably the finest California Cream Sherry.
* Paul Masson: Madeira. When you compare prices on Madeiras, this is a great buy.
* Almadén: Tinta Ruby Port. A very good after-dinner drink, made by the solera system.
* Ficklin: Tinta Port. Compares favorably with other Ports that sell for as much as $25.
* Paul Masson: Rare Tawny Port. Very good for the money. All of Masson's so-called "Rare" dessert wines are excellent buys: Rare Dry Sherry, Rare Cream Sherry, Rare Flor Sherry, and for something different, the Rare Souzao Port.
* San Martin: Aprivette. Made from apricots, it is unusual and extremely sweet.
* San Martin: Sum Plum. This one is so sweet it substitutes for pie and cake after dinner.

IMPORTED WINES

Australia

*Lindeman: Claret (Private Bin). Hearty and full of bite; it needs four to five years of aging.
* Lindeman: Porphyry. This wine is very much like a French Sauterne.

Greece

* Achaia Klauss: Roditis Rosé. Very different for a rosé, owing to the kind of cask used for aging.

Portugal

* Alianca: Rosé. Has an unusual character all its own. A full quart costs less than a fifth of comparable wine.

* Vinya: Rosé. Although we like Lancer and Mateus Rosés, we think they are too expensive. Vinya is a better buy.

Israel

* Adomatic: Dry Burgundy. Inexpensive, and different from any other country's Burgundy.

* Carmel: Sauvignon Blanc. Very tasty, but not like a California Sauvignon Blanc. Worth trying.

Spain

* Marques de Riscal: Rioja. Spanish wines are not our favorites, but we do recommend this red generic.

* Cascante: Cabernet Sauvignon. Interestingly different from other Cabernet Sauvignons. All the varieties in this wicker-wrapped series are good buys.

Italy

* Mirafiore: Bardolino. Similar to a Chianti in body, but much smoother.

* Bolla: Valpolicella. This is the aristocrat of the more common Italian red wines.

* Brolio: Chianti (Flasks). Brolio has established a reputation for good quality control. We are told the wicker-covered "flask" bottle will soon be priced out of range, but you can buy Chianti in a plain bottle just as easily, though you will lose a bit of Old World charm.

* Bolla: Soave. A good tasting, medium-priced Italian white wine.

Germany

As we have stated earlier in this chapter, we suggest you get started on German wines by buying those imported by reputable shippers. We recommend both the Havemeyer brand and the Julius Kayser brand, whichever is available in your area, for both are recognized as importers of quality wines at reasonable prices. Another acceptable brand, if the above are not available, is Beameister.

For your purpose as a beginner there are two types of German wine that should concern you—Moselle and Rhine. There are other types, as you may know, but we emphasize the phrase, "for your purposes." Save your curiosity about other types until you have more expertise.

Moselle and Rhine, as you know by now, are wine-producing regions in Germany. Most of these wines, in fact by far the majority of all German wines, are made from the Riesling grape, but the area in which the grapes are grown determines the character of the wine they produce. Our suggestion is that you try **97** two Moselles and two Rhines, dividing them up between the brands as we indicate.

Moselle

* Havemeyer: Bernkasteler Riesling. Now available in the 1970 vintage, but buy what you can.
* Julius Kayser: Piesporter Riesling. One of our favorite wines, regardless of price.

Rhine

* Havemeyer: Johannisberg Riesling. Quite different from California versions of this wine.
* Julius Kayser: Rüdesheimer Riesling. The vintages of 1970 and 1971 are preferred, but purchase what is available.

Two other German wines that we like very much, and which seem to be asked about frequently are:

* Julius Kayser: Zeller Schwartz Katze. A Moselle type which we do not hesitate to recommend.
* Blue Nun: Liebfraumilch. One of the most popular German wines sold in this country; although this brand is a bit high in price, it is drier than most Liebfraumilchs and we appreciate that.

Once you have experienced these basic German wines, trust yourself to move on to some of the estate-bottled varieties. At first stay with the Moselles and Rhines, but as your confidence increases expand your buying to include wines from the other areas. You will soon be knowledgeable and able to make choices that suit your palate.

France

As we did with wines from Germany, we recommend that you begin buying French wines by brand names. The two labels we suggest you start with are Armand Roux and Barton and Guestier, the latter usually referred to as simply B&G. Both assure you of good quality at a fair price, and both are available in almost all sections of the United States. Thus, for our Burgundy and Bordeaux listings we have omitted the brand name; either of these two brands will be acceptable. For example, when we name Pouilly Fuissé as a favorite white Burgundy, you can assume that both the Armand Roux brand and the B&G brand are recommended. After beginning in this manner and getting your feet wet, so to speak, we think you will soon be able to move on to château bottlings without much fear or intimidation, because you will know, more or less, what to expect from a given variety.

The two best-known wine-producing regions in France are Burgundy and Bordeaux, as you have already learned, and we recommend that neophytes limit themselves to these two. There are, of course, many other wine-producing regions, as well as a multitude of subdivisions of subareas within the two main areas, and it gets complicated very quickly. Two areas that are trying to establish a separate identity are Beaujolais and Côtes-du-Rhône, and we have therefore listed one of our favorites from each.

99

BURGUNDY

* Pouilly Fuissé. This is the best-known and most accepted French white, Chablis excepted. It is good, but unfortunately the price fluctuates, and the higher prices do not mean better wines.

* Pinot Chardonnay. A very dry white Burgundy, quite different from the wine of this name from California.

* Nuits-St.-Georges. Our favorite of the medium-priced red Burgundies. Velvety with a slight bite.

* Mâcon Rouge. Another red that we find pleasing. You might try both brands of this as your first comparison.

* Pommard les Epenots. Buy the newer vintages and hold them until they are about ten years old; it will be a good investment for both your palate and your pocketbook.

BORDEAUX

* Médoc. Our number one choice among the red wines of Bordeaux. Médoc is the name of a region, not a grape.

* Margaux. Another region and another excellent red, which we like almost as well.

* St.-Emilion. A third red we recommend. All of these red Bordeaux wines are best in the 1970 and 1971 vintages, many experts claiming that those were the best years since 1959.

* Graves Supérieur. A white Bordeaux from Graves, and our favorite of that type.

* Haut Sauterne. You will find this quite different from any California Sauterne.

* Barsac. A sweet white wine that, while different from any other, is approximated by California Dry Semillion.

RHÔNE

* Château de la Gardine: Châteauneuf-du-Pape. Many better wine shops carry this red wine, and it is not overpriced, as so many Châteauneuf-du-Papes are.

BEAUJOLAIS

* Martin LeVeque: Beaujolais. An excellent version of the red wine from Beaujolais; we like it young, with no more age than it has at the time it is released for sale.

There you have it—our favorite wine list. But remember, that is all it is; *our* list of *our* favorites. It will be like no one else's, and personal preferences being what they are, there will be those who firmly disagree with some of our choices. There is nothing wrong with that. We offer it in the hope that it will serve as a starting point for you as you learn for yourself which wines you like and which you dislike. And soon, we feel sure, you will be able to make up a list of your own favorites.

Blending & Making Your Own Wine

The attitude many wine experts and wine snobs take toward a bottle of wine might lead you to believe there is something holy about what is inside the bottle. Wine *has* been called "the nectar of the gods," you know, but too many people take that phrase too literally; wine is delightful, terrific, magnificent, but it is of *this* world, not some other one.

Wine snobs carry over this awe-stricken attitude to the realm of blending and making wine, intimating that none but a chosen few are capable of competence in this area. That is simply not true. Almost anyone can blend or make some very nice wine.

Certainly blending and making wine on a commercial scale are complex procedures; no one could say otherwise. In order to stay in business a winery must produce a lot more wine than you would ever consider producing at home, and to do that it needs special techniques, special equipment, and a special know-how.

Here is one way it might go in a commercial winery. The grapes are harvested over a three-week period and the initial sugar content is measured. After de-stemming, an automated procedure, the grapes are crushed and placed in roto tanks, where they are fermented at 76° for four and one-half days. Part of this fermentation—the free-run juice—is put aside with some of the grape skins, then stored for about three weeks in order to produce more tannins, body, and varietal characteristics. This batch is finally pressed, innoculated with malo-lactic bacteria, and further fermented. The other portion of the skins is pressed immediately, the malo-lactic bacteria is added, and this is fermented for another four days. Finally, both portions are separately centrifuged into new sixty-gallon oak barrels for aging. In approximately two years the two wines are blended according to the cellar-master's expert taste, filtered, then bottled. An analysis is made of the wine, and the total alcohol, acid, and sugar percentages are determined. When the winery deems it appropriate, the wine is released to the market.

If the procedures sound scary, do not be put off. It is not necessary to have all that technical equipment to make wine, nor is it necessary to go through all those complicated processes. The home winemaker and the commercial winery have different goals in mind, and they must therefore go through vastly different steps.

The same idea holds true for blending wine. It is one thing to do it at home, quite another to do it on a commercial level. Yet for some reason the wine industry has made such a noise about the techniques of wine blending that the mere thought of it scares **104** people off; they begin to think they cannot do it at home. Absolutely not true; you *can* blend at home, just as many fine restaurants blend for themselves. They buy wine in bulk, blend it, and come up with their own house wine.

As far as commercial blending is concerned, it is a tricky business, and the people who are charged with this responsibility have wine palates developed to an uncanny degree. They can taste a given wine and tell you just about all there is to know about that wine's pedigree.

The coffee industry has similar expert tasters, people with palates so finely honed that they can tell from the taste what percentage of Colombian, what percentage of Bolivian, what percentage of whatever, is in that coffee. And because there are these different blends, and therefore different-tasting coffees, most people prefer one or two brands of coffee over all the others.

So it is with wine and wine blenders. You will prefer one blend of Burgundy over another simply because they contain different percentages of the different varieties of wine, and your palate agrees more with one cellarmaster's taste than it does with another's.

It is our opinion that California winemakers are much better at blending than the winemakers of any other region or country. As we have mentioned in an earlier chapter, they seem to be able to blend for consistency so well that the same wine from the same company tastes pretty much the same over a period of years. For example, a generic Burgundy from the "Ajax Wine Company" will taste practically the same in 1976 as it did in 1975. One year they may use 30 percent

Zinfandel in their blend, but the next year, to achieve the same taste, they may have to use 50 percent Zinfandel. This is where they excel, in producing the consistent taste.

The Christian Brothers Winery, by the way, has a reputation for being the best blender of all, and even its varietals are fairly consistent in taste from year to year. In other words, its Cabernet Sauvignon will taste the same two years from now as today.

Blending Wine

Do not allow all this to frighten you away from trying to blend your own wines, for on the home level the process is not nearly as complicated as on the commercial level. Remember, you are blending for your own taste only, not for the taste of the general public. Even Fred Sanford, of the television show "Sanford and Son," blends his own wine—Fred drinks Ripple wine with a touch of cream added to it. He calls it "Cripple"!

We think you will agree that is quite a blend. Yet it does bring up an important point; do not be afraid to experiment. You can't make anything poisonous by blending different wines, assuming that all the wines were okay to start with. No mixture of wine will make you ill unless it has turned to vinegar, in which case it is easy to spot before you drink too much because it will taste and smell like vinegar! So try a few ideas of your own. You may discover an original blend that will become your favorite wine.

106   We recommend that you jot down on

paper all the recipes you try, so that when you blend something particularly suited to your own palate you will be able to duplicate it whenever you want. Measure the proportions as you mix them, either by percentages or fluid measure (ounces, pints, quarts), and also note the brand and type of each wine you use. You will then have a recipe to follow the next time you want to blend something similar.

We further suggest that you use inexpensive wines when you begin, buying them in either half-gallons or gallons. But do not mix all of them at one time; start in small quantities, so that in case you do not like what you have blended, you will not have wasted a lot of wine—and money. When you blend something you don't like, which is almost unavoidable, don't throw it away too quickly. Experiment a bit. You can blend an infinite number of wines together. Add a few ounces of something unusual and see what you come up with. You may like it.

Nor should you think that the wine you have left over from blending, say the quart of Burgundy you did not mix, has to be consumed immediately, as the wine industry often suggests. We have had California Burgundy last for two to three weeks in the refrigerator, and Chablis last for longer than that. You just do not have to drink it all up in one sitting. French wines, on the other hand, will not last as long after being opened, in our opinion a result of the beating they take in their travels. Those you should try to use within a week.

Now for a start: we suggest you begin by blending for a Rosé. You may remember that many Rosés, except for the varietal types like the Grenache Rosé, are blends of red and white wines. So to make your Rosé, combine Burgundy and Chablis in equal parts, 50 percent of each. This should give you a dry, fairly heavy Rosé.

If this blend is too dry for your palate, give it a slightly sweeter finish by reducing the Burgundy about 10 percent and replacing it with a sweet Rhine wine. Then adjust the blend from this point, adding or subtracting according to your own taste buds. That is really all there is to making a fine Rosé.

Although many people prefer their white wines quite dry, you may find that you like a finish to them. It is quite simple to blend for your individual preference if you are having trouble finding a white wine that exactly suits you. The trick is to use a wine slightly drier than you like for the bulk of your blend, adding small portions of a sweet white wine to it until the mixture is correct.

Similarly, red wines can be slightly sweetened with the addition of another wine, if you cannot find one suitable. A very nice Burgundy blend, which some of our friends like, is made by adding a touch of Madeira. This gives the Burgundy a slightly nutty flavor. How much Madeira to add is a moot point; it depends upon your tastes. Start by adding a small percentage, say around 5 percent, and increase it until you are pleased with the results.

There is another reason for blending red

wines—in our opinion a more important one

than sweetening them. You will recall that many red wines improve with age—Burgundy, Claret, and Bordeaux, to be more specific. As a beginning wine aficionado, however, it is easy to become impatient waiting for the necessary time to pass. Sure, you would like to know what well-aged Burgundy tastes like, but you can't afford to buy it already aged, and you don't want to wait the two or three years or longer for the younger stuff to grow old.

Blend a little well-aged wine with a lot of young wine to improve the latter

There is a technique for making younger wines age faster than they would if you simply allowed nature to take its course. This aging technique is to blend an older wine with a young one, something commercial wineries have done for years.

You will need something to mix the wine in, preferably not metal (to avoid the risk of imparting a metallic flavor to the wine), that will hold about five gallons. Pour four gallons of a young and inexpensive Burgundy into the container, then add one fifth of a very good Cabernet Sauvignon that is from five to seven years old, or one fifth of a good Zinfandel that has been aged that long. Mix well—do not just pour it together and expect something to happen—but mix gently. Rebottle the mix in the gallon jugs, taking care to fill each jug all the way to the top, so there is no room left for air. Once the jugs are filled to the brim, slip some wax paper inside the cap and screw it down tight.

The portion that will not fit into the gallon jugs can be funneled into the fifth bottle and used within the next few days, but store the jugs of your blend at room temperature for at least a few weeks, and a couple of months if you can. What will happen is that the older wine will cause the younger Burgundy to age more rapidly than normal, and when you open one of the jugs at the end of the aging period you will have a very nice, decently aged Burgundy. It will be better than the original jug wine for the price of a fifth of the good and well-aged Cabernet Sauvignon or Zinfandel.

Occasionally a bottle of wine will spoil, either because it was stored improperly or because it was not consumed soon enough after opening. But as we said before, the only way wine spoils is by turning to vinegar. It takes about a month for the change to begin, and at least two to four months for the change to be complete. By all means, do not throw spoiled wine into the trash. Save it and use it, for it will be wine vinegar, just what you buy in the supermarket.

If wine has started to change into vinegar, but is not there yet, you can divide it into two bottles and store it with the cap off. This allows more oxygen to get to the liquid and hastens the process.

Another method, and the one we use, is to keep an open crock (though covered with cheesecloth) in the pantry or kitchen, just for making vinegar. Any wine left over from dinner that we do not want to save for drinking, say two or three ounces, we pour into this crock. It "marries" with the vinegar already there and soon becomes part of it. But a word of caution: add only table wines to the mixture, not dessert wines. Save the dessert wines for cooking.

A film, or skin, called the "mother of vinegar," will form on top of the liquid. When you want to use some of your vinegar, just skim this film aside and take what you need. Do not remove this "mother of vinegar," for it is an integral part of the continuing process of change.

Actually, vinegar itself cannot spoil, and the older it is the better. In certain gourmet shops you can pay as much as $20 for a bottle of vinegar, simply because it is old— like thirty-five to forty years old! In fact, many of your grandmothers probably kept a five-gallon barrel of vinegar "working" for years. So if you keep your vinegar crock working all the time, you can have "gourmet" vinegar at no cost, since you will have made it from wine you would otherwise have thrown away.

As an aside while we are discussing vinegar, you might be interested to know that an old folk medicine recipe for a facial cosmetic calls for using vinegar and rose petals. According to the believers in folk medicine, an integral part of your skin's chemistry is acetic acid, which is removed when you wash your face with soap and water. Because vinegar *is* acetic acid, a facial cleanser made from vinegar is supposed to be good for your skin. The recipe calls for boiling a pint of vinegar with a handful of rose petals, straining and bottling it, and then aging it for a few weeks before cleansing your skin with it. We have no idea about the value of all this, but we certainly find it interesting.

Having gotten off the track of blending wines, let us get back on by mentioning one final blend and a few more general hints. Certain people find that the strong characteristics of Sherry and of Port are too much for their palate to handle, but that a mixture of the two is quite to their liking. They make an appetizer or dessert wine by mixing nearly equal parts of each. It is an extraordinary blend, but who is to say it is wrong if someone likes it? That is exactly what we mean when we urge you to experiment.

If you can use your imagination a bit, you may find that you can save a bottle of wine you would otherwise discard or relegate to the vinegar jug. Suppose you open a bottle of wine and discover that you do not like it at all. Going a little further, suppose you dislike the wine so much that you simply do not want to drink it. Before you throw it away, try blending this wine with another wine you like better. You can change the character of a bottle of wine with just a few ounces of something else, and you may find that you have blended a wine that is quite suitable for your taste buds, and have therefore "saved" it.

Of course it is possible that you could begin with two wines you like moderately well, and in blending them come up with one that you do not like at all. It can, and does, happen. All we can say to that is, do not be discouraged, and follow our original advice of starting in small quantities. That way blending becomes fun, and you do not have to concern yourself with wasting a lot of money. Then, once you hit upon a blend you like, you will be far ahead of the game.

Making Wine

It is important for you to realize right off the bat that as complicated as commercial wine-making is, making wine at home is fairly simple and straightforward. Yet even though home winemaking is much less sophisticated, it works. All you have to do is follow our recipe and you will produce some very good wine.

If you try our way and find that you enjoy making your own wine, there are a number of books on the market that treat the subject more thoroughly. Their recipes will differ slightly, and they may suggest alternate procedures which you would find more to your liking; so if you get interested and want to make more than the few gallons we talk about here, we suggest you consult a few of these books to increase your knowledge and your competence. Your local library will undoubtedly have copies of many of them. But for now, try it our way.

Quite naturally the first step in making wine is to procure some grapes. You can grow your own, which is perhaps the most fun, or you can buy them. Depending upon how much wine you want to make, and therefore how many grapes you need, there are several ways to buy grapes. Local stores will probably order what you want, if you do not want too many. You can also go to the produce yard of your city and buy grapes directly from the wholesaler. If you decide to go into wine-making on a larger scale, the best place to get grapes is from the grower.

We really cannot tell you what variety of grapes to buy, because that depends upon what is available in your area. Almost any grape will make wine, including the Thompson Seedless, the Concord, and any of a hundred varieties. If you can, buy a wine grape (any produce man will know, or can find out, what suitable varieties are available to you); but do not be put off if you can't.

Fortunately for home winemakers, there is a shop run by Mr. Bob Ellsworth, called "The Compleat Winemaker," where you can buy all the equipment and supplies you will need. He publishes a catalogue, which he will

send you, and he handles mail orders as

promptly as possible. He does not sell grapes. The address of the shop is:

The Compleat Winemaker
1201 Main Street
St. Helena, California 94574

The first piece of equipment you will need is a fermenting barrel. It can be plastic, stone crockery, or wood. We prefer a fifty-gallon oak barrel, but use whatever you can find. If you use something you are not sure about, you can buy plastic liners for your container and throw them away after each use. If there has been *anything* stored in your barrel you will have to clean it thoroughly before you use it. Fill it with warm water and dissolve in it two pounds of baking soda or soda ash for each fifty gallons of its capacity. Allow this mixture to stand for a day or two, then scrub the barrel vigorously. The baking soda not only cleans the barrel, it also neutralizes any acids that might be present, and this is important because the acids could spoil your wine. If you are using a wood barrel, the soaking will swell the staves and insure that the barrel is watertight.

An advantage to the wood barrel is the ease with which the liquid can be drawn off through the spigot. Ideally this spigot will be located a few inches from the bottom, so that when you draw off the wine, the sediment remains undisturbed at the bottom of the barrel, and therefore out of the wine. If you use a container that has no spigot, you will have to siphon, pump, or pour the wine from the container, and somehow filter out whatever sediment gets into the wine. Our advice is to search long and hard for a wood barrel

Blending
& Making
Your Own Wine

115

with a spigot before turning to something else. And while larger barrels may be scarce, smaller ones are not too hard to find and barrel spigots are cheap.

Stomping the grapes is the best way to crush them

With some grapes and a clean barrel on **116** hand, you are ready to begin. The first step is to crush the grapes and, lacking a wine press, the easiest way is to stomp them. Scrub a pair of rubber boots as scrupulously clean as you can, remove the leaves from the grape clusters, dump the grapes into a tub, and stomp! If you cringe at the thought of stomping your grapes you can use a wood paddle of some sort, but believe us, it's a lot easier to stomp them—and a lot more fun!

Whatever you do, do not wash the grapes. You have learned that the white substance on the skin of the grape is yeast. As you crush the grapes and break the skin, the yeast will mix with the sugar inside the grapes and cause them to ferment. You need the white substance (yeast) to make things work.

Once you have broken the skins, pour the mixture into the fermenting barrel, filling it only three-fourths full (so the fermenting mixture does not overflow). Cover the open top of the barrel with cheesecloth or some other type of screening to keep out insects. It is a rule of nature that fruit attracts flies, and believe us, fermenting fruit attracts more flies; so place your fermenting barrel away from your house. But do not worry; if a few flies accidentally fall into the barrel, they will not contaminate your wine.

For the next week or so there is a task that you simply have to perform, and that is to agitate the mixture (called the "must"). The agitation must be done gently; mix gently at the beginning and mix gently all the way through. Very soon after you begin, the grape pulp and skins and stems will rise to the top of the barrel, floating on the liquid beneath.

117

This is called the "cap." Using a wood (not metal), paddle or tamper, gently push the cap down into the must, thereby mixing the yeasts and sugars for better fermenting. You should do this two or three times daily.

Homemade paddle to push the cap down into
the fermenting mixture

Approximately a week after you begin, the wine will be done fermenting. The way to tell when is to study the bubbles. When there are no bubbles rising freely, and when no more than about ten bubbles per minute rise when you push the cap down, your wine has fermented.

Carefully skim off the cap—the skins, the stems, and any leaves that may have sneaked into the mixture—so that you disturb the wine as little as possible. This is to keep the sediment on the bottom where it belongs.

The next step is to clarify your wine, which you can do either before or after drawing it from the barrel. The old way to do this was to use egg whites, beaten stiff enough to float, and covering the entire surface of the wine. They would settle to the bottom, taking with them any sediment that was in the wine. But it is a messy, messy process.

The same thing can be accomplished with isinglass or gelatin, but we have found that two or three layers of cheesecloth work as well as anything for the home winemaker. Commercial wineries, of course, use extremely sophisticated filtering systems (cellulose pads, asbestos pads, diatomaceous earth, mini-micron filters), but they generally agree that a minimum amount of filtration is best. Over-filtration can rob a wine of its natural body and its varietal characteristics. The use of cheesecloth eliminates this worry for the home winemaker.

The next procedure is to bottle or cask the wine. The choice is yours, but make your choice with the thought in mind that wine ages about twice as fast in wood as in glass. If you have some smaller casks available, we urge you to use them. You will have a nicer wine for doing so. Just be sure that the casks are sealed tightly.

Whether you bottle your wine right after clarifying or after aging it in wood for a while, the steps are the same. Make sure the bottles are absolutely clean, and be certain the cap or cork is airtight. If you use old corks it pays to put some wax paper over them so there is no chance of contamination from old wine. If you use new corks remember to store the bottles on their sides so the corks will stay moist and swelled. Screw-on caps just have to be put down tightly. Fill each bottle completely, so there is very little space for air, seal it, label it, and you are done.

You can make one addition to the above recipe, if you so desire, and that is to add a stabilizer to the wine. Sometimes we do, more often we do not, but now you are the wine-maker and it is up to you. A stabilizer insures that the wine will age, rather than spoil, and it does not affect the taste of the wine one iota. You simply add one teaspoon of cream of tartar for every gallon of wine before you bottle. Try making your wine both ways, with the stabilizer and without, and see what effect it has before permanently deciding to use it or not.

To further stretch the yield from your grapes, it is possible to squeeze some additional wine from the stems and skins left over from the first batch. This involves adding sugar, yeast, and water to the cap from the original batch, and then following the procedure as before. This wine will be drinkable, but it will not be nearly as good as the original, and we do not recommend it.

If you have grown your own grapes and find that you have too many for the size of your fermenting container, do not think they will be wasted. Simply leave the excess grapes on the vine until you are ready to use them. They will keep better that way than if you picked them and tried to store them. The worst that can happen is that the grapes will dry out a bit and begin to look like raisins. If so, they can still be used for wine; just add some water when you start the fermenting **120** process.

Fruit Wine

Fruit wines are made in much the same way as grape wines, but because other fruits do not carry their own yeast, you must add it. You do not need sugar, however, because all fruits have their own sugar, though you may find that the addition of a small amount will make the wine more palatable. The proportions are variable, depending upon which fruit you are using. We have found that, in general, it takes about four cakes of yeast dissolved in water for about forty gallons of berries. Because you are supplying the yeast, rather than it coming from the fruit itself, it is important that you mix everything well. You also may find that home-made fruit wines are too acid for your taste, in which case some water should be added. Unfortunately, the water should be added during the fermentation, not afterwards, and because you cannot taste the wine and learn anything until it is fermented, you will not know how much water to add until it is too late. You can take a guess at it, adding two or three pints of water for every ten pounds of berries, but remember it is an estimate and you will have to adjust for your own tastes in subsequent batches.

If you find that your fruit wine is not sweet enough for your taste, *do not* add sugar after the fermentation is complete unless you are prepared to pasteurize each bottle. We do not recommend such a procedure, as pasteurization can be fairly tricky, but instructions for the process can be found in the references below.

Legal Aspects

Home winemaking is subject to certain legal restrictions.

* The producer must be the head of a family household of more than one person.

* The producer must reside with his family.

* The winemaking must not be contrary to state law.

* The wine must not be furnished to persons not members of the producer's family.

* The producer should file two copies of Form 1541 with any regional office of the Internal Revenue Service before starting production.

References

As you can see, making wine at home is a fairly easy proposition. Remember, you are not a commercial winery and you are not in mass production. The whole idea is to have some fun while you make some good wine.

But home winemaking is like many other hobbies in that is appeals to some and not to others. If it turns out to be fun for you and you do take it up as a hobby, you should investigate the subject more thoroughly. We suggest you begin that investigation with a small booklet called Wine Making at Home, by Maynard Amerine and George Marsh. It is distributed by Vintage Press, P.O. Box 2470, Yountville, California, 94599. You will find it a concise and factual explanation of some of the more intricate steps in home winemaking. Amerine has also authored (in some cases co-authored) a number of other books on this and related subjects.

Other selected references (and this is by no means an exhaustive list) are:

HARDWICK, HOMER, *Winemaking at Home.* New York: Cornerstone Press, 1974.

TAYLOR, W.S., and VINE, R.P., *Home Winemaker's Handbook.* New York: Harper and Row, 1968.

TRITTON, SUZANNE, *Guide to Better Wine and Beer Making for Beginners,* 2nd ed. New York: Dover, 1969.

Cooking with Wine

Most wine aficionados firmly believe that nothing enhances a good meal like a good wine. What many of them do not know is that a good recipe is almost always enhanced by the addition of some wine to the list of ingredients. Wine adds its own special character to a dish, just as the spices and other ingredients you use add their own character.

Perhaps the cardinal rule in cooking with wine is, *use a light touch.* For the housewife or the Sunday chef, or for anyone who is unfamiliar with using wine in his or her cooking, we must advise that it can easily be overdone, especially with Sherries and the other dessert wines.

How many times we have experienced the disaster of beginning gourmet cooks as they scatter spices hither and yon over their food, completely obliterating the flavor of the dish they are trying to prepare. Contrast that to the attitude of experienced gourmets, who use their spices and flavorings gently, subtly, in an effort to enhance, not to disguise. Cooking with wine is a parallel situation. You simply must be discreet.

The basic proportion that you should

begin with when cooking with wine is to substitute wine for one-half of the liquid called for in the recipe (that is, unless the recipe itself already includes wine). In other words, if your recipe calls for two cups of water, use one cup of water and one cup of wine instead. It is that simple, and you can adjust to your taste as you experiment. But do not use these proportions with dessert wines, for they are more dominating and must be more lightly dispensed.

The obvious question now is, what kind of wine should you use? There are various theories about that. Somehow word has gotten out that you should only cook with a wine you would serve to your guests. That is to say, if you are serving a $5 bottle of Burgundy with your meal, you should cook with some of that $5 wine. To us, that is nonsense.

It is nonsense because what you are seeking when you cook with wine is flavor, *not* character, quality, bouquet, alcohol, or the mellowness that comes from aged wine. All of these are cooked away, and what remains is the flavor of the wine. In our opinion the only reason for using expensive wine in cooking is to increase the profits of the wine companies—no other. The flavor—not the quality, but the flavor, remember—of good inexpensive wine is little different from the flavor of expensive wine. So use the cheaper stuff. We have never found that using the higher-priced wines makes any difference in recipes; so you will never catch us adding a $5 bottle of Burgundy to our beef stew. We will use the cheaper jug wines.

It is important, however, to use the same kind of wine in cooking as you will serve with dinner. If you are serving that $5 bottle of Burgundy with your meal, use a Burgundy wine in your recipe. The flavor of one will enhance the other. If you use, on the other hand, one type of wine in cooking and then serve another type with the meal, the flavors will fight each other and your meal will be less than the success it could have been.

Likewise, there is a reason for the old rules about which wine to serve with which dish. The rule is general: it says to serve red wines with red meat, and white wines with fish and fowl. The reason is compatibility. The wine and the food should complement each other so there is a harmony between food and drink.

On the other hand, do not be afraid to experiment. We happen to enjoy immensely a light red wine with a breakfast of pancakes and maple syrup. It is an uncommon idea, one that many wine experts would call crazy. But we like it, we enjoy it, and so we indulge ourselves.

You will remember from the chapter on wine-tasting parties that we said you must serve the lighter wines first, because you do not want to overpower your palate with the heavy ones before you sample the lighter ones. With meals it is perfectly acceptable, even adventurous, to serve more than one wine, but it is crucial to know in what order to serve them. And the order is the same as it was for wine-tasting parties; first white wines, then rosés, and finally the reds.

If you want to serve wine with the salad

course, we recommend a light white wine. Some people like a bit of Champagne with their salad, but we do not, as we feel the "bubbly" will affect your taste buds and limit your enjoyment of both the meal and the other wines. Finally, about half an hour after dinner, you can conclude your meal with fruit, cheese, and a dessert wine, perhaps some Sherry.

It would also be tasteful to begin with a rosé—that is, to serve it with the salad—and then follow it with the red wine. Or, you might serve white wine with the salad and a rosé with the main dish, if that is what you like. The important point to remember is that under no circumstances should you serve the heavier and stronger-flavored wines first; you will only destroy your taste for the lighter and more delicately flavored wines.

Those, then, are the general rules. We hope you will be inspired to try some of the following recipes, and to experiment further on your own. And because everyone who has ever hosted a party is on the lookout for a punch recipe, we are starting off with our recipe for fruit punch.

FRUIT PUNCH

⅕ of a quart (a fifth) Mai Tai mix
1 can (46 oz.) apricot nectar
1 can (46 oz.) pineapple juice
1 can (24 oz.) guava nectar
1 can (24 oz.) papaya juice
2 cans (48 oz. total) chunk pineapple
2 fifths Brandy

A few hours before the party mix all the fruit and fruit juices with the Mai Tai mix, add ice, and allow to chill. Just before serving add the Brandy, mix well, and garnish with mint, gardenias, or roses.
Serves 40, 1½ cups apiece.

BEEF ROAST

¾ cup red wine
¾ cup water
4-lb. or larger beef roast
oregano, thyme, pepper, garlic (to taste)

Punch deep holes on both sides of the roast with a knife. Blend together the wine, water, and spices, and allow this mixture to sit for an hour or two. Then pour the mixture into the holes in the roast, catching any overflow, which you will use for basting. Preheat oven to 350°. Cook for prescribed length of time: rare—19 minutes per pound; medium rare—21 minutes per pound; well-done—23 minutes per pound. Baste frequently. Use pan drippings for sauce and gravy.

OTHER ROASTS

Follow the basic procedure for beef roasts, using red wine with veal, lamb, venison, and game birds, but using white or rosé with a pork roast. Remember to serve the same type of wine you cook with. To pork roasts, we add a touch of sage.

HEARTY BEEF ROAST

As a special treat try this sometime. To the **129**

spices and wine and water mix of the basic beef roast recipe, add a coffee mixture of 2 tablespoons of instant coffee dissolved in 1 cup of boiling water. This does *not* give your roast a coffee flavor, but it does add a rich, hearty brown flavor that blends well with the wine.

MARINADES

Add some red wine to your favorite meat marinade. The acids and tannins in the wine will not only flavor the meat, they will also tenderize it.

SPAGHETTI SAUCE

To your regular spaghetti sauce recipe, add a dry red wine like a Chianti, a Burgundy, or a Zinfandel. It is possible that you will find the higher acid content objectionable. If so, after the sauce has been cooked about half the total time, add some baking soda to it to neutralize the acidity. The baking soda will not alter or kill any flavors, but it will add smoothness, sweetness, and creaminess.

CHICKEN BREASTS

1 boned chicken breast
2 slices prosciutto ham
¼ cup grated Gorgonzola cheese
½ cup Sherry or Madeira
¼ lb. finely sliced mushrooms
1½ tbs. butter
salt and pepper to taste

Pound the chicken breast flat after cutting

it in half, so that you have two patties. Place a layer of ham over the patty, then sprinkle with the Gorgonzola cheese. Roll up and hold with a toothpick. Salt and pepper to taste, then sauté in butter until brown on both sides. Add the Madeira or Sherry, spread the mushrooms on top, and place in a medium oven (350°) in a covered pan for 15 to 20 minutes. To serve, place on a dish and spread the mushrooms and wine from the pan over the top. A variation on this dish is to substitute veal for the chicken, and then you should use Marsala instead of Madeira or Sherry.

VEAL SCALLOPINI

If your veal scallopini recipe is in the Italian style—that is, spicy—add a red wine to it. Otherwise, add a white wine. For a meatless dish, try substituting eggplant for the veal.

GROUND BEEF

Any ground beef recipe, including the ubiquitous hamburger, will be improved with the addition of some red wine.

TUNA FISH CASSEROLE

To any basic recipe for this dish, add a small amount of Sherry or a slightly larger amount of Chablis.

BAKED FISH FILLETS

Fish fillets are usually baked in a butter and lemon sauce. Try adding some white wine to the sauce. To serve, spoon the pan drippings **131**

over the fish and garnish with slivered al-
monds.

OTHER FISH AND SEAFOOD DISHES

Bouillabaisse, clam chowder, shrimp dishes,
and even curries are more complete with a
touch of Sherry or white wine added to them.
You must be careful with the Sherry, however, because it has a strong flavor that can
easily overpower the dish.

EGGS MADEIRA

8 eggs
¼ cup plus ½ tsp. Madeira
8 large or 16 medium-sized mushrooms
Parmesan cheese
butter
salt and pepper
Lawry's seasoned salt

Put the mushrooms in a baking dish,
stems up. To each mushroom add ½ teaspoon
of Madeira, placing it in the cup of the mushroom cap. Place a pat of butter on the stem,
sprinkle with Lawry's seasoned salt, and bake
in a moderate oven. When the mushrooms are
about done, melt ½ stick of butter in a glass
baking dish on top of the stove, and add ¼
cup of Madeira. Place the eggs sunnyside up
in the baking dish and cook until the white is
firm enough to hold its shape when moved.
Sprinkle with Parmesan cheese, and continue
cooking in the oven until the eggs are done to
taste.

Serve the eggs and the mushrooms together, with bacon, Canadian bacon, or small breakfast steak. The wine for this brunch could be a Gewürztraminer, a Grey Riesling, or Champagne. Serves 4 to 8 people.

GRAPEFRUIT APPETIZER

Grapefruit halves
Brown sugar
Sherry or Madeira

Mix a tablespoon of brown sugar with a tablespoon of the wine. Pour this mixture over a grapefruit half, then bake in the oven a few minutes, until the sugar melts. Serve warm. If you are in a hurry, simply pour a teaspoon of Cream Sherry over a grapefruit half, allow to stand for five minutes, and serve cold.

DESSERTS

There are many ways to use wine in your desserts, and the few ways we mention here do not even scratch the surface of the subject. An imaginative use of wine can turn very ordinary desserts into outstanding ones.

One of our favorite desserts is red wine poured over peaches. Ice cream can be enhanced with a touch of Sherry or one of the other dessert wines. Plum wine poured over mandarin orange slices or pineapple slices makes a very easy, but quite tasty, dessert. You can also pour one of the Japanese plum wines over fruit salad and serve that at the conclusion of your meal.

We hope we have given you some idea of   **133**

how to cook with wine. Because our aim is
merely to introduce the subject to you, we are
stopping here before this becomes a recipe
book rather than a wine book. For some excellent recipes that use wine, we recommend
The Store Cookbook, written by Bert Greene
and Denis Vaughan. It not only contains some
great recipes, it is delightful reading as well.

Appetizer &
Dessert Wines

The wines we have discussed throughout most of this book have been table wines, so-called because they are generally served with food. There is another class of wines which we have mentioned, but only in passing, that could be called—for the lack of a better term—non-table wines. Non-table wines are appetizer, dessert, and sparkling wines.

The word *aperitif* is a French term for wine that is taken before meals to stimulate the appetite, but many *aperitifs* (appetizer wines) serve admirably as dessert wines, and therefore the categories are not all that rigid. Dessert wines, likewise, are not to be limited to after-dinner consumption; some of them are quite good at other times. Sparkling wines go well with dessert, can be served with a meal, though we do not like them then, and are the crowning touch to many celebrations of one kind or another. As a matter of convenience, we will refer to them all as dessert wines from now on.

Dessert wines are usually higher in alcoholic content than table wines, though not always, and their sweetness precludes their being served with meals. Not only will they distort the flavor of the food, the food will likewise distort the flavor of the wine.

It is unfortunate that dessert wines are not served more often; they seem to have fallen from grace these days for many people. Sherry, for example, is often thought of as a drink for "little old ladies," who while away their afternoons sipping it from delicate cut-glass wine goblets. Port brings to mind scenes of fat old men with cigars, lounging in a wood-paneled English drawing room after dinner. And many people seem to limit their enjoyment of Champagne to weddings, christenings, bar mitzvahs, and other times of celebrations. All in all, a deplorable situation.

Our suggestion is that you try these dessert wines before you ignore their existence. Try them before dinner or after, but try them. They will provide a highly enjoyable experience that does not have to be expensive.

Brandy

Without a doubt, one of our favorite drinks is Brandy. Nothing pleases us more than to relax after dinner with an ounce or so of Brandy in a glass, which we slowly drink a sip at a time.

Brandy is unusual in that it is made by distilling a certain kind of normally fermented grape wine. That is, the first step in making Brandy is to make wine, and the second step is to distill that wine, just as one distills grain mash in order to get whiskey.

The process of distilling is essentially one of boiling and condensing. In the case of Brandy, the wine is boiled, the steam coming off the boil is routed through tubing, the tubing coils are chilled so the steam condenses into liquid, and the resulting liquid is the distilled spirit—raw, unaged Brandy.

There are two basic methods of distilling Brandy, and we mention them only because occasionally it is claimed that one method is superior to the other. The "pot still" method simply means that the Brandy producer distills one pot of wine at a time. With the "continuous still" method a continuous supply of wine is fed into the boiling vat so that the process is ongoing. As far as taste and quality are concerned, we know of no advantage of one method over the other.

Incidentally, if this mini-description of the distilling process reminds you of moonshiners and revenue agents as you have viewed them in the movies, you have the right idea. It is the same process, only on a much more sophisticated—and legal—level.

Brandy is aged in wood after it is distilled, and the wood, of course, is what gives this drink most of its distinctive flavor. As with all wines, there are variables that affect the final result: age in the cask, the amount of care in handling, and, naturally, the quality of the original ingredients. But it is a common mistake, no doubt fostered by the wine snobs, that the older a Brandy is, the better. The truth is that most Brandies reach their peak long before the thirty or forty years the wine snobs feel is necessary, and it is a great error to think otherwise.

Another common mistake is to think that Cognac is a grade of Brandy, the highest grade. That is not true. Cognac is Brandy that comes from the Cognac region of France, and only the Brandies from that area can right-fully be called Cognacs. There is another region, Armagnac, in the south of France, that also produces exceptionally fine Brandies, and although most wine experts prefer the Brandies from Cognac, we happen to prefer the Armagnacs.

When buying Cognac you will often see some initials on the label that supposedly indicate the age of the Brandy. V.S.O. (very superior old) refers to Brandy that is twelve to seventeen years old; V.S.O.P. (very superior old pale) refers to eighteen- to twenty-five-year-old brandy; V.V.S.O.P. (very very superior old pale) is twenty-five to forty years old. These initials have been assigned over the years as a matter of practice, not as one of legal requirement, so we do not assume their accuracy.

In any case, nowhere in the United States do we produce a Brandy that comes anywhere near the French Brandies in quality. For some unfortunate reason, domestic Brandies are never as smooth, and they are never as pleasing, as those from Cognac and Armagnac.

Furthermore, it appears that some of the world's finest Brandies are not even available in our country. A close friend of ours, a member of the judiciary, had dinner a few years ago at Fernand Pont's *La Pyramide,* considered by many to be the finest restaurant in all of France. Being a devotée of fine Brandy, he asked for a serving of a well-known and highly respected Cognac by name. When the *garçon* turned up his nose at the judge's selection, our friend threw himself open to suggestion. He reported that he was served the finest Cognac he has ever tasted, bar none, and that he has not found its equal to this day.

While you may not be able to sample that particularly exquisite Cognac, we urge you to try both the Cognacs and Armagnacs that are available to you. They will provide a pleasure you should not miss. Brandies, like all dessert wines, are meant to be taken in small doses, to be sipped at leisure with a good book or in good company. The Brandy snifter, in which Brandy is traditionally served, has a definite purpose, which is to allow the Brandy to be slightly warmed by the heat of your hand, and to collect the aroma of the Brandy in the upper portion of the glass. Brandy may also be served in a small cordial glass, providing it is served at *warm* room temperature—that is, around 70 to 75°.

Sherry

Sherry may be served as an appetizer wine, a dessert wine, or both. We facetiously call Sherry "spoiled wine" because of the way it is made. If any other wine were treated the way Sherry is treated, it would indeed be spoiled. But this special treatment, along with the type of grape that is used, is what gives Sherry its distinctive nutty flavor.

Usually fermented from the Palomino grape, Sherry wine is subjected to heat to produce its character, either in a baking oven or room, or in barrels that are placed outdoors in the sun. The Sherry can remain in one barrel until it is ready, or the winery can use the "solera" system.

The solera system is a method of aging that blends young wines and old wines together. The process is a valid one that is similar in theory to one of the blending techniques we told you about in Chapter VIII. We liken it to a grandfather taking his grandson by the hand and leading him through some of the more difficult periods in his life. The way it works with Sherry is that the barrels of wine are stacked in tiers, with the newest wine on top and the oldest at the bottom. When the bottom barrel of Sherry is ready for bottling, only about one-half of it is drawn off. That barrel is refilled from the barrel immediately above it, which in turn is topped off from the barrel above it, until unaged new wine is needed to fill the uppermost barrel. It is an old system and not in much use today, but Almadén still makes its Sherries this way and produces some very nice wines for the price range.

While this heating and aging process is what gives Sherry its distinctive flavor, its nutty taste, individual Sherries vary widely. They range from "flor fino" Sherries, which are the very driest, to "oloroso" Sherries, which are quite sweet, and almost every degree of sweetness in between. The well-known and popular "cream" Sherry is one of the sweeter ones.

We suppose that because of advertising, one of the most famous Sherries is Harvey's Bristol Cream from Spain. Harvey's also produces dry and semi-dry Sherries, but the advertising campaign has seemingly concentrated on the Bristol Cream. There is no doubt that it is excellent, but it is also expensive; we feel that Gallo Livingston Sherry is almost its equal, and we certainly find the enormous price difference hard to justify. A second very good and inexpensive cream Sherry is Gold Label Meloso Cream Sherry from the Christian Brothers Winery.

Another type of Sherry is Amontillado, which is usually very dry. You may recognize the name from Edgar Allan Poe's short story, *The Cask of Amontillado.*

A cousin to the Sherry is Marsala. Marsala is a bit sweeter and not nearly so dominating in flavor, but it has lost popularity in the United States and is now used chiefly in cooking. That is a shame, for it is quite good.

Because of its nutty flavor, Madeira might be called another cousin to Sherry. Madeira ranges from fairly pale and dry to quite sweet. The dry is called *sercial*, the semisweet *boal*, and the sweetest *malmsey*. It is said that Madeira was George Washington's favorite drink, and in this bicentennial era it is certainly worth a try.

Port

Port wine seems to lend itself to snobbery better than almost any other wine. Its mention does serve to remind you of the days of the noble gentry so aptly described in English literature.

But Port is not to be easily dismissed, and we find it an excellent drink before dinner or after, and also at bedtime. Port originally came from Portugal, as its name implies, and is a heavy-bodied wine, rather **141** sweet to the taste, ranging in color from ruby to tawny.

While it is true that Ports, like Sherries and Madeiras, need a great deal of aging time to reach their peak of flavor and quality, there is a considerable difference of opinion as to how much is enough. Where dinner wines are concerned, aging time ranges from a few months to a few years, with a few notable exceptions like the Pommards. But the frame of reference for aging Ports is much longer— from ten years to fifty to one hundred.

We doubt the necessity of the extremes, and we also doubt the value of them. Obviously it is the consumer who must pay for the long periods of aging, and we personally do not think that the price difference between a ten-year-old and a fifty-year-old Port coincides with any increase in quality, at least as far as the average person is concerned. Most of our palates simply could not appreciate the minimal difference.

For example, Harvey's Director's Bin Port is generally considered to be one of the finest in the world, and it certainly is well-aged; but we have found that Gallo's Tawny Port is not far off in taste and quality, and it is a lot less costly.

So as we have done from the start with all wines, we recommend that you try some of the inexpensive Ports first, then gradually work your way into the costlier versions. And if you find that you cannot tell the difference between the low-priced ones and the high-priced ones, by all means buy the inexpensive ones. But do try one or two Ports; we would hate for you to miss out on this traditional pleasure.

Sparkling Wines

Sparkling wines are fun, quite tasty, and add to the enjoyment of almost any occasion. Indeed, there is nothing quite like the excitement that is generated from opening a bottle of Champagne or Sparkling Burgundy, hearing the cork "pop!", and watching the delicate bubbles foam in your glass. But it is too bad that a lot of us limit our consumption of sparkling wines to special occasions, for we miss out on a great deal of fun.

The most common sparkling wines in the United States are Champagne, Sparkling Burgundy, and Cold Duck. Spumante, the Italian answer to France's Champagne, is not so well known here. Wines with just a hint of effervescence are called *crackling* wines in this country, *pétillant* in France, and *fizzante* in Italy; and aside from Paul Masson's Crackling Rosé they are not too popular.

The word "Champagne" is the name of a region in France, and according to French law wine may be called Champagne only if it is made from grapes grown in that region. American-made Champagne, therefore, is not actually Champagne, but rather a copy, but we have broadened the term in actual usage so that it now means sparkling white wine. If the French will forgive us, which we doubt, we will use the word "Champagne" in its broadest sense.

Sparkling Burgundy is basically nothing **143**

more than red Champagne; that is, an effervescent red wine that has characteristics similar to Champagne. Cold Duck is almost always a simple blend of one-half Champagne and one-half Sparkling Burgundy, and there are those who enjoy it more than the pure versions of either. We do not, however, because we think it lacks the good qualities of both its ingredients. But that is our taste, and you should rely on your taste, so do not let us dissuade you from something you like.

Champagne is produced from a variety of grapes, the principle ones being the Pinot Chardonnay, a white grape, and the Black Pinot, or Pinot Noir. Because the pigment of the latter grape is all in the skin, care is taken to ensure that none of the coloring (or at least as little as possible) gets into the press of the wine. The result is a white wine, rather than a red one.

After the grapes are pressed, the original fermentation takes place, producing an ordinary, or "still" wine. Additional grape sugars and special yeasts are then added to the still wine and a second fermentation occurs; this second fermentation is what produces the "bubbly." There are two ways to achieve it. It can be done in bulk, as is the case for inexpensive Champagnes, or it can be done in the individual bottles, a more expensive procedure. The second fermentation causes gas bubbles (CO_2) to be trapped within the wine, and this is the effervescence you see when Champagne is poured. Finally the bottle is racked for aging, and it is released to the market when the Champagne is ready to be consumed.

We believe that Champagne should be drunk at this point, without further aging. In our opinion, aging Champagne beyond "winery time" is a refinement to be tried only by those who have special equipment and facilities, and if you do not have them you should not try it. What is certain is that Champagne will spoil, and our way to keep it from spoiling is to drink it. Therefore, we would never buy more Champagne than we could use within a month or six weeks.

In general you will find that French Champagne has a more earthy character than the American version. Of the Champagnes produced in the United States, those from New York more closely approximate the French style. That is not to say that California Champagnes are inferior, only that they are different, although there are a few that have that European touch.

With regard to French Champagne, the driest is called *brut*, the next driest *extra-sec*, then *sec*, and finally the sweetest is called *demi-sec*. This is the only time the French use the word *sec* (dry) in this way. You will discover, however, that even most brut Champagnes have an edge of sweetness to them, and American-made brut Champagnes will be even sweeter yet. Americans seem to prefer it that way. In any case, the point is that there are distinct differences between French and American Champagnes, a fact you will soon discover for yourself.

The most famous Champagne of all is probably Dom Perignon, named after the French monk who is dubiously credited with

145

inventing this sparkling wine. Mumm's is the choice of many, owing in part to the difficulty in locating Dom Perignon, while Tatinger, Piper Heidsieck, and Charles Heidsieck are other well-known brands that are imported from France. As far as which you should buy, our favorite may not be yours, and it is really a matter of paying your money and making your choice.

The finest of the California-made Champagnes, in our opinion, comes from Korbel. Of the New York state versions we prefer Taylor's over the Great Western brand, but again that is an individual preference in taste and is not meant in any way to downgrade Great Western. We also enjoy Inglenook's vintage Champagne; it has an Old World character we find particularly inviting.

Most American Champagnes are classified as either "brut" or "extra-dry," the former being the driest. Do not be surprised, however, if you prefer the slightly sweeter "extra-dry"; most American tastes seem to run that way. Our personal taste in Champagne is for it to tickle the nose, perhaps even bring a tear to the eye. We do not like the heavy bitterness of some Champagnes, but that is our personal preference and you certainly may like what we do not. As we have said many times, only *you* can make the decision about what *you* like.

Vermouth

Many people do not realize it, but Vermouth
146 is a wine. It is quite different from other

wines though, because it is wine that derives its unique character from the addition of herbs, spices, and other aromatic substances. There are two basic types of Vermouth: French and Italian. French-style Vermouth is dry and usually a pale amber in color, and the American version is usually labeled "double-dry," à la Paul Masson, or "extra-dry," or "triple pale dry," as Almadén calls it. Whatever it is called, dry Vermouth is the second ingredient in a martini, and today not many people drink it without gin.

Italian-style Vermouth is sweet and dark amber in color, and is one of the ingredients in a Manhattan cocktail. But sweet Vermouth is also very tasty served on the rocks with a twist of lemon peel—quite nice as an appetizer.

Liqueurs

Although many of them are not wines, and therefore do not fall within the scope of this book, we want to say a few words about liqueurs. There are a zillion of these after-dinner drinks, some wines, some Brandies, and some simply mixtures of alcohol and flavorings.

Fruit wines, such as the tasty plum wines of Japan, are the result of the fermenting process, but because the grape is the only fruit that carries its own yeast, the manufacturer of fruit wines must supply yeast to his crushed fruit. Apple wines and berry wines are made in this manner.

147

Certain fruit Brandies are made in a similar fashion, with the resulting wine then being distilled, as grape Brandy is. Some other Brandies are produced from grapes, but are handled in such a way that they have a flavor quite different from regular Brandies, and therefore are "liqueurs" rather than true Brandies. The well-known Metaxa Brandy from Greece is one such case; Metaxa is a brand name, not a wine type, and Metaxa Brandy obtains its distinctive flavor from being aged in cedar casks.

Most liqueurs, however, are made by adding flavorings to a base of grain neutral spirits (relatively pure alcohol, or vodka). The flavorings can be oranges, cocoa, coffee, anise, or even Scotch whiskey. You probably are familiar with many of the names: Kahlua, Galliano, Chartreuse (both Green and White), Drambuie, and a host of others.

Many people find it a very simple thing to blend liqueurs at home, using vodka as the base and adding different flavorings. You can come quite close to the commercial brands if you are willing to do some experimenting, and we think it might be fun for you to try it.

A liqueur that we blend at home, and one you might start with, combines the following:

1 pint vodka

5 cups sugar

5 cups water

1 tbsp. banana extracct

½ tbsp. anise extract

yellow food coloring

Simply blend these ingredients together, adding enough food coloring to please your eye, allow to stand for a week or so, and then enjoy. You can, if you wish, use 200-proof grain alcohol instead of the vodka, but you must use the *extracts* of banana and anise, not merely the flavorings. If you keep this liqueur in a nice decanter, you will have an elegant means to end an evening.

Rating Your Wines

The whole idea of this book has been to help you—the beginning wine drinker—find some wines you enjoy at a price you can afford. After a while, after you have sampled numerous types and brands of wine, you will invariably reach a point when your memory will fail and you will forget about some of the wines that you truly loved. Someone will mention a brand of vintage Cabernet Sauvignon, ask your opinion of it, and you will not be able to remember whether it was the San Martin brand or the Louis Martini brand that you liked so well. Being mortal, such things happen to us all.

The way to overcome such indications of human frailty is to keep a written record of your evaluation of every wine that you sample. We do it, the experts do it, almost everyone who loves wine does it.

Evaluating wines—that is, judging and rating them—can be either a very simple process or an extremely complicated one, depending upon what you want to accomplish. On the one hand, the cellarmaster at a commercial winery must make some very expert, detailed, and critical judgments about his wines. You, on the other hand, in your personal judgments, can rely more heavily on subjective likes and dislikes. Certainly you can be much more general in your approach.

There are many ways to rate wines. You could rate them by simply noting that such-and-such a wine was poor, acceptable, or good. You could go to the other extreme and rate every wine on a scale of one to one hundred.

For those with experience in wine evaluation, the system developed by the faculty of the University of California at Davis works well. They have developed a twenty-point scoring system, allotting points on the following basis:

Appearance	2
Color	2
Aroma and bouquet	4
Acescence (vinegar aroma)	2
Total acid	2
Sugar	1
Body	1
Flavor	2
Astringency	2
General quality	2

After rating the wine in question by allotting it points in each of the categories, the judge adds the points and comes up with a sum that is the wine's numerical rating. An absolutely

perfect wine would receive a score of twenty,

while any wine scoring below, say, twelve would be unacceptable.

The University of California system is a good one, but we feel it is too complex for home use. We have therefore, distilled a simplified approach from all the rating systems, in which we observe four basic characteristics of a wine, include the additional factor of price, and then rate the wine on a scale of one to ten. The four characteristics are color, body, smell, and taste.

Color

The color of wine can—but does not always—indicate something about its quality. In white wines we look for varying shades of yellow, gold, or straw; amber tones indicate a flaw to us. In Rosé wines, the "pinkness" can vary, but it should not be tainted with either amber or purple. For red wines the general rule is, the heavier the color, the heavier the wine; so if you get a light red taste out of a deep-colored wine, something is amiss. The color of red wine depends almost entirely on the variety of grape used, but in any case amber tones are an indication of oxidation and are undesirable. In all wines, of course, we look for clarity and brilliance, but we remind you that plain grape juice can be clear and brilliant, too.

Body

The second characteristic to observe is the wine's body. While the body of any liquid ranges from watery to thick and creamy, the terms used for wine are "light" to "heavy." But all judgments about body are relative, not absolute. To observe the body of a wine, swirl the wine in glass and watch what happens on the walls of the glass. Heavy wines will form a "sheet" as they slide down the sides, while "light" wines will form streaks or "tears." For example, we like the body of Cabernet Sauvignon to be heavy, so we want it to "sheet" on the glass; if it "tears" we feel something is wrong. Conversely, a Chenin Blanc, which most of us want extremely light, should form "tears"; if it does not we know it will be too heavy.

Smell

The third characteristic is again judged before you even taste the wine. It is smell, which is divided into two parts, aroma and bouquet. Simply stated, aroma is the grape scent, and bouquet is the winemaking (vinification) scent. Once again we swirl the glass, further aerating the wine and releasing more of the smell, then we place our noses as far inside the glass as we can and take a whiff. What we want is simply a pleasant smell. We do not want any mold scents, or vinegar scents, nor do we like an excessive "woodiness." If we find any of these, we downgrade the wine.

Taste

154 What rating wines is all about, in our opinion, is this final category—taste. Perfect color, perfect body, delightful smell, all are for naught if the wine fails to please our palate.

Because the taste buds are aligned on the tongue in a particular order, and because there are only four basic tastes—or combinations thereof—that you can experience (sweet, sour, salt, bitter), wine tasters have developed a way of tasting that calls for a slight bit of manipulation.

Take a bit of wine in your mouth, pooling it in the cavity between your lower teeth and your tongue. Dip the top of your tongue, where the sweet taste buds are located, into the wine. Next, roll some of the wine over the top of your tongue to the back in order to taste any bitterness. Then, let the wine trickle down the sides of your tongue where the salt (front) and sour (back) taste buds are found.

Finally, aerate the wine by sucking air through it so that you get a huge burst of the overall flavor throughout your entire mouth. Try not to be embarrassed about the slurping noise you have just made!

With a little practice you will be able to separate fairly well each of the distinct tastes of sweet, bitter, salt, and sour. With the final rush of flavor that comes from aerating the wine in your mouth, you can then make an overall judgment of the taste of the wine.

The Rating

The final step is to assign a numerical rating to the wine you have tasted. We do not allot so many points for each category, as in the University of California system. We take into

155

consideration all the factors of color, body, smell, and taste, then add the subjective factor of how much we liked the wine as we drank it. Then we consider the price factor, handling it in this way: it we taste two wines that are very similar and that please us equally, yet one is $7 a bottle and one is $3, we give a higher rating to the cheaper one because we are interested in value as well as taste.

Thinking about all these things, we give the wine a numerical rating from one to ten, ten being the highest and reserved for a perfect wine.

Most likely you will start off rating many of your wines fairly low. That is the result of years of intimidation by the wine snobs. You will soon discover, though, that some of the wines with a good reputation rate no better by your tastes than some of the much cheaper ones. All you have to do is adjust your rating scale to your own tastes, so it better fits you.

How do you use this scoring record? Our own policy is fairly simple. For home use, we buy only those wines with a rating of six or above. Anything below six we forget for a couple of years, or until such time as we have reason to taste it again. On the other hand, remember that your tastes will change as time goes by; so if you think that has happened to you, try some of your previous low scorers. You may be pleasantly surprised. Naturally we urge you to determine for yourself what is the lowest rating a wine can have and still be of interest to you. Perhaps you will not buy any wine that scores under seven; it is up to you.

We use the form on the following pages for our records, and we have included a few blanks for your use. The form is simple and self-explanatory.

Wine	Price	Date bought	Date used

Comments	Rating

Wine	Price	Date bought	Date used

Comments	Rating

Wine	Price	Date bought	Date used

Comments	Rating

Glossary

Alicante Bouschet (Ah-lee-CANT Boo-SHAY). A staple grape in Burgundy blends; also used in home winemaking.

Alsace (Al-SAYCE). The French province on the Rhine, noted for spicy white wines.

Amontillado (Ah-mon-teel-YAH-do). A type of dry Sherry.

Aperitif (Ah-pair-ee-TEEF). A beverage taken before meals to stimulate the appetite.

Appellation Contrôlée (Ah-pay-lah-SEEOHN Kontroll-AY). Words supposed to indicate geographical truth on French wine labels.

Armagnac (AR-man-yak). A Brandy-producing region in France.

Auslese (OWS-lay-zeh). A German term; wine so indicated is made from selected bunches of grapes.

Barberra (Bar-BAIR-ah). A red wine grape and a varietal red wine.

Barsac (BAR-sack). A sweet white wine from Bordeaux of the Sauterne type.

Beaujolais (Bow-shaw-LAY). A light red wine from a district in Burgundy.

Beerenauslese (BAY-ren-ows-leh-zeh). A German term; wine so indicated is made from individually selected berries of selected bunches.

Blanc de Blancs (Blonh de blonh). A white wine made from white grapes.

165

Blanc de Noir (Blonh de nwahr). White wine made from black grapes, primarily Champagnes made from Pinot Noir grapes.

Blanc Fumé (Blonh Few-MAY). A white wine grape and a varietal wine; *see also* Sauvignon Blanc.

Bordeaux (Bor-DOUGH). A city and region in France; the major wine-producing districts in Bordeaux are Médoc, St.-Emilions, Pomerol, Graves, and Sauternes.

Bordeaux Rouge (Bor-DOUGH Roozh). Generic red wine from grapes grown anywhere within the Bordeaux region.

Botrytis Cinerea (Bo-TRY-tis Sin-eh-RAY-ah). A natural mold that concentrates the grape sugar; often called the "noble rot."

Brut (Broot). A relative term, indicating dryness; in France it refers to the driest Champagne, in the United States to a slightly sweet Champagne.

Cabernet Sauvignon (Cah-bear-NAY So-veen-YONH). A red wine grape and a varietal red wine.

Carignane (CARE-een-yanh). A red wine grape, used mostly in blends.

Chablis (Shah-BLEE). A generic dry white table wine, named after the region in France; also, a white Burgundy.

Chambertin (Shawm-bair-TAN). Red wine from a vineyard in the Côtes-de-Nuits region in Burgundy.

Charbono (Shar-BONE-oh). A red wine grape and a varietal red wine.

Chardonnay (Shar-dun-NAY). A white wine grape and the proper name for Pinot Chardonnay; thus a white wine.

Château (Shah-TOE). An estate lending its name to a wine.

Châteauneuf-du-Pape (Shaw-toe-NEWF dew POP). Red wine from a chateau in the Rhône Valley.

Chenin Blanc (Cheh-NANH Blonh). A white
wine grape and a varietal white wine.

Chianti (Key-AUNT-ee). A red wine, Italian in
character.

Claret (CLAIRE-et). Red Bordeaux-type wine.

Cognac (KON-yak). A Brandy-producing region
in France.

Colombard (Coll-om-BARD). See French Colombard.

Côte-de-Beaune (Coat-d'BONE). The southern
part of the Côte-d'Or region in Burgundy.

Côte-de-Nuits (Coat-du-N'WEE). The northern
part of the Côte-d'Or region in Burgundy.

Côte-d'Or (Coat-d'OAR). The large area in the
center of Burgundy, divided into Côte-de-
Nuits and Côte-de-Beaune.

Côtes-du-Rhône (Coat-du-ROWNE). Red wine
from the Rhône Valley in France.

Crackling (KRACK-ling). A wine just slightly
effervescent.

Cuvée (Ku-VAY). The blend of still wines used in
making Champagne and other sparkling wines.

Entré deux Mers (On-TRAY dir MAIR). A large
district in Bordeaux producing white wine.

Fino (FEE-no). A term applied to light-colored,
fairly dry Sherry.

French Colombard (French Coll-om-BARD). A
white wine grape and a varietal white wine.

Frizzante (Free-ZAHN-tay). The Italian term for
crackling wine.

Gamay (Gah-MAY). A red wine grape and a
varietal red wine.

Gewürztraminer (Geh-WIRTS-trah-meen-err). A
white wine grape and a varietal white wine.

Graves (GRAHV). A white wine from that region
in Bordeaux.

Grenache (Gren-AHSH). A wine grape used to
make Rosé wines.

Grignolino (Green-yo-LEEN-oh). A red wine
grape and a varietal red wine. **167**

Haut (OH). The French word for "high," which is used in the United States to mean "sweet."

Lambrusco (Lahm-BROOCE-coh). A frothy red or white wine; the Italian answer to Spanish Sangría.

Liebfraumilch (LEEB-frow-milsh). A white wine from Germany.

Loire (L'wahr). A region in France along the Loire River.

Mâcon (May-CAWN). A region in southern Burgundy.

Madeira (Mah-DARE-ah). A dessert wine.

Margaux (Mar-GO). Wine from the Margaux parish in Médoc.

Marsala (Mar-SAH-lah). A dessert wine that is sweeter than Sherry and Madeira.

Médoc (MAY-dock). Claret (red) from this district in Bordeaux.

Merlot (Mare-LOW). A red wine grape.

Meursault (Meer-SOH). A township in the Côte-de-Beaune in Burgundy.

Montrachet (Mawn-rah-SHAY). A white Burgundy wine.

Moscato Canelli (Moe-SCOT-oh Cah-NELL-ee). The Italian name for one of the Muscat grape varieties.

Moselle (Mo-ZELL). White wine from the Moselle River district in Germany; similar California white wine.

Muscadet (Muss-kah-DETT). A dry white wine from the Loire Valley.

Muscat (MUSS-kat). A white wine grape.

Muscatel (MUSS-kah-tell). Sweet dessert wine made from the Muscat grape.

Nebbiolo (Neb-ee-OH-low). An Italian sparkling wine.

Nuits-St.-Georges (N'wee-San'h-Zorzhe). Red wine from this village in Côte-de-Nuits in Burgundy.

Palomino (Pal-oh-MEEN-oh). A white wine grape used in making Sherry.

Pétillant (PET-till-awnt). The French equivalent to "crackling."

Petite Sirah (P'TEET Sear-RAH). A red wine grape and a varietal red wine.

Pinot Blanc (PEE-no Blanh). A white wine grape and a varietal white wine.

Pinot Chardonnay (PEE-no Shar-doe-NAY). A white wine grape and a varietal white wine; see also Chardonnay.

Pinot Noir (PEE-no NWAHR). A red wine grape and a varietal red wine; the grape has white juice within the red-black skin and is sometimes used to make Champagne.

Pomerol (POM-er-all). A district in Bordeaux producing red wine.

Pommard (POH-mar). Red wine from this township in the Côte-de-Beaune region of Burgundy.

Pouilly Fuissé (POO-ye Few-SAY). White wine from the Macon area in southern Burgundy.

Puligny Montrachet (Poo-LEEN-yee Mawn-rah-SHAY). A township in the Côte-de-Beaune region of Burgundy; thus, a wine from there.

Riesling (REEZ-ling). A white wine grape and a varietal white wine.

Rosé (Roe-ZAY). Pink table wine.

St.-Emilion(s) (San'h Eh-mee-YONK). A district in Bordeaux producing red wines; also a white varietal wine from California (rare).

Sancerre (Sawn-SAIR). White wine from the Loire Valley.

Sangría (Sahn-GREE-ah). A mixture of wine and citrus juices, originally from Spain; now a generic name.

Sauterne (So-TAIRN). A white wine type, named after the Sauternes district in Bordeaux.

Sauvignon Blanc (So-veen-YONH Blonh). A white wine grape and a varietal white wine, often called by other names; for example, Blanc Fumé.

169

Schloss (Schlawss). The German equivalent to *château*.

Sec (Seck). A French word meaning "dry"; in the United States it means "sweet."

Semillon (Say-me-YONH). A white wine grape and a varietal white wine.

Soave (SWA-veh). An Italian dry white wine.

Sommelier (So-mel-YEAH). A wine waiter; holder of the key to the wine cellar.

Spätlese (Shpayt-LAY-seh). Wine made from grapes picked late in the season.

Spumante (Spoo-MAHN-tay). A sparkling wine from Italy; the Italian term for "sparkling."

Sylvaner (Sill-VAN-er). A white wine grape and a varietal white wine.

Traminer (Trah-MEEN-er). A white wine grape and a varietal white wine.

Trockenbeerenauslese (Trock-en-BAY-ren-ows-leh-zeh). A German term indicating the time of grape picking, in this case when the grapes are overripe and almost raisins. Compare Spätlese, Auslese, and Beerenauslese.

Valpolicella (Vahl-po-leh-CHEL-lah). A red wine from northern Italy.

Vermouth (Ver-MOOTH). Wine flavored with herbs and spices.

Vin (Vanh). The French word for "wine."

Vosne Romanée (Vone Roe-MAN-nay). A red wine from the Côte-de-Nuits area of Burgundy.

Vouvray (Voo-VRAY). Wines produced in the Loire Valley region of France; generally the white wine of that township.

Zinfandel (Zin-fan-DELL). A red wine grape and a varietal red wine from California.

Index

Rüdesheimer Riesling, 98

St. -Emilion, 29, 85, 100
San Martin
  Aprivette, 95
  Sum Plum, 95
Sauterne, 32, 35, 85, 101
Sauvignon Blanc, 92, 96
Sebastiani
  Pinot Noir, 88
  Sylvaner Riesling, 90
Sec, 19, 145
Sediment, 68, 115, 118
Sherry, 94-95, 112, 131, 132, 133, 136, 139-41
Soave, 36, 85, 97
Solera system, 139-40
Sommeliers, 72-75
Souverain Green Hungarian, 91
Spaghetti sauce, recipe for, 130
Spanish wines, 96
Sparkling Burgundy, 143-44
Sparkling wines, 94, 135, 143-46
Spätlese, 36, 50
Spoilage, 64-67, 110-11
Spumante, 86, 94, 143
Stabilizer, 120
Store Cookbook, The (Green and Vaughan), 134
Storing wine, 59-65
  red wines, 60-63
  white wines, 63-64
Sum Plum, 95
Sylvaner Riesling, 90

Tatinger Champagne, 146
Tavel Rosé, 37-38
Taylor
  Champagne, 94, 146
  Lake Country Pink, 38
  Lake Country Red, 28, 93
Temperature changes, wine and, 8, 10, 60-62
Tinta Port, 95
Tinta Ruby Port, 95
Traminer, 33
Trockenbeerenauslese, 50
Turnover, 10-11

Valpolicella, 30, 85
Varietal wine, defined, 18
Vaughan, Denis, 134
Veal scallopini, recipe for, 131
Vermouth, 146-47
Vin ordinaire, 25
Vinegar, 65-66, 111-12
Vintage, 8, 53-56
Vinya Rosé, 96
Vouvray, 35

Waugh, Harry, 28
Weibel
  Chenin Blanc, 91-92
  Green Hungarian, 91
  Moscato Spumante, 94
Wente Brothers
  Blanc de Blancs, Le, 84, 91
  Dry Semillon, 91
  Petite Sirah, 93
  Sauvignon Blanc, 92
White wine, 31-36
  aging, 36, 63-64
  Australian, 95
  blending, 108
  Californian, 31-33, 90-92
  French, 31, 34-36, 100-101
  German, 33-34, 97-98
  Israeli, 96
  Italian, 36, 97
  storage, 63-64
Wine
  aging, *see* Aging process
  alcoholic content, 40-42
  appetizer wines, 94-95, 112, 135-49
  authors' favorites, 87-101
  blending, 104-13, 148-49
  care of, 8-9, 59-70
  cooking with, 125-34
  descriptive terms, 19-22
  dessert wines, 41, 42, 94-95, 112, 126, 135-49
  generic names, 18-19
  glasses, 78-79
  labeling, *see* Labeling
  making, 103-4, 113-23
  naming of, 18-19
  ordering in restaurants, 71-76

175